READING AND INTERPRETING THE BIBLE SERIES

DANIEL

BARRY L. ROSS

f▸

THE FOUNDRY
PUBLISHING®

The Foundry Publishing®
PO Box 419527
Kansas City, MO 64141
thefoundrypublishing.com

ISBN 978-0-8341-4169-8

Printed in the
United States of America

Cover design: Caines Design
Interior design: Jody Langley/Sharon Page

Library of Congress Cataloging-in-Publication Data
A complete catalog record for this book is available from the Library of Congress.

10 9 8 7 6 5 4 3 2 1

Contents

Abbreviations 5

Part I: Introductory Matters... 7

   1. Historical Background....................................... 9

   2. General Features...15

   3. Issues That Influence Your Interpretation 23

   4. Chapter Summaries....................................... 28

   5. How to Read and Interpret the Book of Daniel............41

Part II: Interpreting the Book of Daniel 45

 A. Daniel 1–6: Stories of Daniel and His Friends Hananiah,
   Mishael, and Azariah at the Babylonian Court 47

   6. Story One (Dan. 1)..47

   7. Story Two (Dan. 2) 63

   8. Story Three (Dan. 3).......................................77

   9. Story Four (Dan. 4) 88

  10. Story Five (Dan. 5).......................................102

  11. Story Six (Dan. 6) 116

 B. Daniel 7–12: Daniel's Four Visions for the Future of
   God's People 133

  12. Vision One (Dan. 7) 133

  13. Vision Two (Dan. 8) 152

  14. Vision Three (Dan. 9) 167

  15. Vision Four (Dan. 10–12): God's Final Word
   to Daniel..183

Bibliography 189

Abbreviations

General

cf.	compare
ch(s).	chapter(s)
Gk.	Greek
HB	Hebrew Bible
Lat.	Latin
lit.	literally
n.p.	no page
NT	New Testament
OT	Old Testament
r.	reigned

Modern English Versions

AT	Author's Translations
ESV	English Standard Version
ISV	International Standard Version
KJV	King James Version
NASB	New American Standard Bible
NIV	New International Version
NJPS	New JPS Hebrew-English Tanakh
NKJV	New King James Version
NRSV	New Revised Standard Version

Apocrypha

1–2 Macc.	1–2 Maccabees

PART I

INTRODUCTORY MATTERS

1

Historical Background

The book of Daniel is a very ancient book. It has twelve chapters. Chapters 1–6 tell stories of Daniel at the Babylonian court, serving both Babylonian and Persian rulers. Chapters 7–12 describe Daniel receiving visions from God concerning the future rise and fall of kingdoms.

The Babylonian and Persian Empires

As you can guess, the main human character of this book is Daniel, a Jew from Judah. The events of his life are set within the (Neo-)Babylonian and Persian Empires, beginning in 626 BC. In that year, a royal prince named Nabopolassar defied the power of the Assyrian Empire, taking over rule of the province of Babylon. From then on, Babylonian expansion was unstoppable; within two decades all the former Assyrian-controlled territories were under Babylonian control. Thus began the Babylonian Empire about which the Old Testament speaks.

But in the overview of history, world rulership is fickle. Less than a century later, world dominance passed to the Persians when, in 539 BC, a Persian named Cyrus conquered Babylon, taking control from the Babylonians. Thus began the Persian Empire. This empire expanded until it became geographically the largest known in the biblical world up to that time. It ultimately extended eastward to the edge of India and westward to the edge of Europe. The Persian Empire lasted twice as long as the Babylonian Empire.

But, alas, a Macedonian military general named Alexander the Great brought the Persian Empire to its knees after its two hundred years of world rule. In two great battles in 333 BC at Issus and again in 331 BC at Gaugamela on the northeast Mediterranean seacoast, Macedonian Alexander fought and defeated Persian king Darius III. By 326 BC, Alexander had conquered Persian territories and cities all the way eastward to India.

Daniel's Early Life

Judean Daniel lived more than twenty-six hundred years ago, far removed from our modern times! We have no written details of Daniel's early life. Yet we may speculate that he was born around 620 BC.[1] This would have been during the reign of Judah's righteous king Josiah, who reigned in the last half of the seventh century BC, from 640 to 609 BC. Keep in mind the name Josiah because we'll speak of him again later.

Daniel was born in the ancient land of Judah (see Dan. 1:6), with its capital city of Jerusalem. Judah was located in the same area as present-day Israel, bordering on the eastern seacoast of the Mediterranean Sea. Yet Daniel lived most of his eighty-year life in the ancient city of Babylon, in the south of present-day Iraq.

Throughout the seventh century BC, the period that included Daniel's birth and early life, the power broker of the biblical world was Assyria. The Assyrian armies went out in all directions from the city of Nineveh, located on the Tigris River in northern Mesopotamia, in present-day Iraq. The power of Assyria had influenced life in Judah for decades.

In the decade prior to Daniel's birth, and during the first decade of his life, however, profound changes were taking place that were affecting

---

1. Jim Edlin, *Daniel*, New Beacon Bible Commentary (Kansas City: Beacon Hill Press of Kansas City, 2009), 28.

Daniel's smaller world of Judah. The power and influence of Assyria was declining. This great power was being squeezed and ripped apart by two powerful competing forces: Babylon from the southeast and Egypt from the southwest.

So, how did Daniel, born in Judah, end up in Babylon far to the east?

The Assyrian Takeover of Northern Israel

Here we must go back to a century before the birth of Daniel and the reign of Judah's king Josiah. In 743 BC, Assyrian power from Nineveh, under King Tiglath-Pileser III (r. 745-727 BC), began expanding westward into the kingdoms on the eastern side of the Mediterranean Sea, including Israel. Tiglath-Pileser's practice, after conquering a resistant kingdom, was usually to rename it and then make it a province of the Assyrian Empire. He would deport a significant number of that kingdom's citizens to other Assyrian-controlled lands far away, mixing them with the local populations. A series of Assyrian incursions into northern Israel continued over two decades, until northern Israel and its capital city, Samaria, succumbed to the armies of Assyria in 722 or 721 BC. The Assyrian army deported 27,290 of northern Israel's citizens to far northeastern regions of the Assyrian Empire.[2] The kingdom of northern Israel was absorbed into the Assyrian Empire and renamed the province of Samaria.

What happened in the southern kingdom of Judah over the century following the demise of northern Israel (and much did happen!) does not overly concern us here for the book or story of Daniel. We must note, however, that Assyria continued to rule the biblical world throughout, with Judah existing in a somewhat vassal relationship with Assyrian power.

---

2. John Bright, *A History of Israel*, 4th ed. (Louisville, KY: Westminster John Knox Press, 2000), 275.

The Crowning of Josiah as Judah's King

In an incident of Judean palace conspiracy, in 640 BC, some servants of the then-reigning, idol-worshipping Judean king, Amon, "assassinated him in his palace" (2 Chron. 33:24). Why? The Chronicler does not say. A group of power brokers, whom the Chronicler calls "the people of the land" (v. 25), however, quickly nipped this rebellion in the bud: they killed the conspirators! And though Amon's son Josiah was at the time only eight years old, these power brokers immediately crowned him king in his father's place (33:24–34:1).

King Josiah's Religious Cleanup

When Josiah was sixteen years old, in his eighth year of rule, "he began to seek the God of his [fore]father David" (2 Chron. 34:3). Four years later, in his twelfth year of rule, "he began to purge" all the places of worship from Judah and Jerusalem that his father and other earlier kings had set up in competition with or in place of worship at "the temple of the LORD [*yhwh*] his God" (vv. 3, 8). This purging was no half-hearted affair. Josiah did it violently: he tore down, cut and broke to pieces, smashed, scattered, burned, and crushed high places, Asherah poles, altars, bones, and idols. He then extended his religious cleanup northward beyond Judah into the towns of four tribal areas of the former northern Israel: Manasseh, Ephraim, Simeon, and Naphtali (vv. 3-7).

At this time, as mentioned earlier, Assyrian power was declining, leaving somewhat of a power vacuum in Judah and the Assyrian province of Samaria (the former northern Israel). Neither of the other two wannabe replacement powers, Egypt or Babylon, had yet won the day for world domination. Josiah took advantage of this power vacuum to expand his religious cleanup into former northern Israel. John Bright interprets this action as Josiah's declaration of independence from Assyrian power.[3]

---

3. Ibid., 317.

After his cleanup action in the north, King Josiah returned to Jerusalem (v. 7) to continue further religious reforms throughout Judah. This included a renovation of the Jerusalem temple and restoration of temple worship. As an interested reader, you would do well to read the details of these reforms in 2 Kings 22:3–23:25 and 2 Chronicles 34:1–35:19. Josiah essentially completed them by about 622-621 BC, but their positive effects continued on into the first decade of Daniel's life.

King Josiah's Death

Tragically, King Josiah's life was cut short a little over a decade later when, in 609 BC, he was killed in a battle at Megiddo while meddling in the great military struggle between Egypt and Babylon for world dominance (see 2 Kings 23:28-30; 2 Chron. 35:20-24).[4] Four years later, in 605 BC, the Egyptian and Babylonian armies fought a great chariot battle at Carchemish on the river Euphrates. The Babylonian army, under the military leadership of Nebuchadnezzar, the son of Babylonian king Nabopolassar, defeated the Egyptian pharaoh Necho, winning the title for world dominance. You can read Jeremiah's poetical account of this decisive battle in Jeremiah 46:2-12, in which Jeremiah names "the Lord, the LORD Almighty" (v. 10 [2x]) as truly the one deciding the outcome of this decisive battle.

Daniel Taken to Babylon

Daniel would have been fifteen to seventeen years of age when Nebuchadnezzar was crowned king of Babylon in late 605 BC, following the death of his father. Soon after this, and continuing until at least 601 BC, he brought his army west and then southward down the Mediterranean seacoast several times, destroying towns in Syria and the Philistine plain.[5] Daniel 1:1 appears

---

4. Ibid., 324-25.

5. Ibid., 326. See also John Goldingay, *Daniel*, Word Biblical Commentary 30, ed. Nancy L. deClaissé-Walford, rev. ed. (Grand Rapids: Zondervan, 2019), 152; Ernest Lucas, *Daniel*, Apollos Old Testament Commentary 20, ed. David W. Baker and Gordon J. Wenham (Downers Grove, IL: InterVarsity Press, 2002), 51.

to reference one of these campaigns of Nebuchadnezzar when the author speaks of Nebuchadnezzar's threat against Judah's capital city, Jerusalem.

It seems that King Nebuchadnezzar continued to do what the former Assyrian king Tiglath-Pileser and other Assyrian kings had done when conquering foreign kingdoms: he selected many of the best of those kingdoms' young men and women, deporting them to Babylon and its environs. There were several possible reasons for doing so. In this context, giving them a Babylonian education and a position in the service of the king was an apparent desire to strengthen the home base with their skills.[6] Though we have no written record of Daniel's selection and journey from Judah to Babylon, the book of Daniel opens with Daniel and three other named "Israelites from the royal family and the nobility . . . from Judah" (1:3, 6) in Babylon in the time of Babylonian king Nebuchadnezzar. These other three are "Hananiah, Mishael and Azariah" (v. 6).

King Jehoiachin's Deportation to Babylon

In 597 BC, some two and a half decades after Daniel was taken to Babylon, Nebuchadnezzar again came against Jerusalem. The current Judean king, Jehoiachin, surrendered. Nebuchadnezzar deported him, his family, and ten thousand Judean citizens to Babylon (2 Kings 24:8-17). Though the book of Daniel makes no mention of this large influx of Jews into Babylon and its environs, Daniel surely would have been aware of them.

An archaeological discovery, an administrative document in the Babylonian language, lists deliveries of oil to various persons dependent on the Babylonian royal household. These included 10 *sila* of oil for Jehoiachin, 2½ *sila* of oil for his sons, and 4 *sila* of oil for eight men from Judah.[7]

---

6. Goldingay, *Daniel*, 154.
7. *Ancient Near Eastern Texts Relating to the Old Testament*, ed. James B. Pritchard, 2nd ed. (Princeton, NJ: Princeton University Press, 1955), 308.

2

General Features

What You Will Read in the Book of Daniel

When you read the book of Daniel, in chapters 1–6 you will read stories about Daniel and his three Judean friends and their involvement in events at the royal Babylonian court. Scholars have called these "court tales."[1] Some of these events are life threatening, a couple highlight religious resistance, and others call on Daniel's insightful ability to interpret royal dreams and visions. Exciting stuff!

None of these tales, however, is truly about Daniel, though on the surface he appears to be the star of the show. Each tale serves to reveal who the God of these Judean foreigners truly is: it is *he* who raises kings to thrones and removes them; it is *he* who ultimately controls the rise and fall of earthly kingdoms; it is *he*, "the God of gods and the Lord of kings," who gives all humans knowledge and abilities; and it is *he* who is "a revealer of mysteries" (2:47).

When you continue reading the book of Daniel, in chapters 6–12 you will read about Daniel's four visions concerning the future. Scholars call

---

1. See, for example, Lucas, *Daniel*, 25.

these visions "apocalyptic," a type of literature that we will explore later. Of these final six chapters, in chapters 10–12, you will read of a great war to take place between two Greek kingdoms—still some three centuries in the future from Daniel's time, but ancient history from our perspective.

Perhaps as you read this ancient book, you may discover that Daniel's God is one who delights in surprises, both then and now. One of these surprises is that though he is the "God of heaven" (Dan. 2:18 et al.), he is one who "can save" as "no other god" in earthly life-threatening situations (3:29).

The Date of the Book of Daniel: Traditional and Nontraditional Views

Traditional

The traditional view concerning the date of writing and who wrote the book of Daniel can be summed up in the following three points:

1. The stories as presented in the book of Daniel are set in the latter years of the Babylonian Empire and the early years of the Persian Empire—that is, in the sixth century BC.

2. The book looks prophetically forward from the sixth century BC to events up to and into the second century BC.

3. A narrator who knew Daniel (perhaps one of his disciples) wrote the book in the sixth century BC or shortly after.

Stephen R. Miller has suggested a completion of the book when Daniel was "an old man soon after the last dated event recorded in the book (10:1; 536 B.C.)."[2] The event referenced in Daniel 10:1 is the "third year of Cyrus king of Persia."

---

2. Stephen R. Miller, *Daniel*, The New American Commentary 18 (Nashville: Broadman and Holman, 1994), n.p., Kindle; see also Edlin, *Daniel*, 241.

Nontraditional

The nontraditional view concerning the date of writing and who wrote the book of Daniel can be summed up in the following points:

1. Generally there is agreement with traditional point number 1 above.

2. The book of Daniel was not *written* in the sixth century BC, but rather, an anonymous Jew wrote it in the second century BC during a Jewish rebellion known as the Maccabean Revolt. This revolt was against the Greek-Seleucid ruler Antiochus IV Epiphanes, who ruled Syria (including Palestine-Israel) from 175 to 164 BC.

3. This anonymous Jewish author wrote the book of Daniel in the mid-160s BC[3] as an encouragement to his beleaguered fellow Jews in their struggle against their Greek oppressors.

4. The book of Daniel, having been written in the second century BC, was not written prophetically. Rather, it was written *historically*, as though it were prophecy. That is, the second-century BC writer looked back to the events of the sixth century, assumed a character named Daniel, and then brought events "prophetically" up to his own time in the second century BC.[4]

This book follows the traditional view on the date and authorship of the book of Daniel.

The Languages of the Book of Daniel

The book of Daniel is written in two related Semitic languages. Daniel 2:4–7:28 is written in Aramaic, a form which scholars call "Imperial Aramaic."[5] This became the official language used internationally throughout the biblical world from about 700 to 200 BC[6] between peoples who spoke

---

3. Goldingay, *Daniel*, 131.
4. Ibid., 98.
5. Ibid.
6. Lucas, *Daniel*, 307.

various Semitic languages and dialects. The remainder of the book of Daniel is written in Hebrew.

The shift in Daniel 2:4 from Hebrew to Aramaic is surely more than a casual stylistic choice on the part of Daniel or the recorder of the material. John Goldingay observes that the insertion of Aramaic, the colloquial language of the Babylonian Empire, into the surrounding text of Hebrew, the literate language of the people of God, is a stunning rhetorical declaration. It is an affirmation that although the people live in a world ruled by an empire, represented by Aramaic, the truth that circumscribes their lives, signified by the surrounding Hebrew text (before 2:4 and after ch. 7), is the dominance of the God of Israel over the words and strength of the empire.[7]

Of interest is that the book of Daniel contains some loanwords from three other languages. There are nineteen from Old Persian, thirty-seven from Akkadian, and three from Greek, which refer to musical instruments.[8]

Aramaic as the International Language

A request for the use of (Imperial) Aramaic occurs in 2 Kings 18:26. In 701 BC, Assyrian king Sennacherib invaded Judea. Jerusalem had closed its gates against this threat. Sennacherib's military general appeared outside the wall and verbally read Assyrian surrender terms in the "Hebrew" (lit. "Judean") language to Judean king Hezekiah's officials. They were on top of the wall and did not want these surrender terms heard by others who were also on the wall. So the Judean officials requested of the Assyrian general, "Please speak . . . in Aramaic, since we understand it" (v. 26). The Assyrian commander scoffed at their request and continued speaking in Hebrew (vv. 27-28).

---

7. Goldingay, *Daniel*, 193.
8. Kenneth A. Kitchen, "The Aramaic of Daniel," in *Notes on Some Problems in the Book of Daniel*, ed. D. J. Wiseman (London: Tyndale Press, 1965), 31-36.

Apocalyptic Literature

Scholars refer to the book of Daniel as *apocalyptic* literature. In Daniel, the term "apocalyptic" primarily applies to Daniel 2 (a dream) and 7–12 (visions).

The term "apocalyptic" is an English adaption of the Greek word *apokalypsis*, which means "revelation." This word occurs in the opening sentence of the New Testament book of Revelation: "The revelation [*apocalypse*; Gk., *apokalypsis*] from Jesus Christ, which God gave him" (Rev. 1:1). Thus, explains Tremper Longman III, "Apocalyptic is a form of divine revelation given to human beings."[9] This is revelation of future events and usually comes in dreams or visions.

Apocalypticism in the Old Testament was not a stand-alone literature with no connection to other types of literature before it or alongside it. Jim Edlin affirms,

[Apocalyptic literature's] connection with prophetic literature indicates that apocalypticism was in some sense a development or extension of the prophetic movement in Israel. Images and concepts used in apocalyptic literature are deeply rooted in Israel's prophetic tradition. Apocalyptic writings also betray connections to Israel's wisdom tradition and non-Israelite sources. Influences from Babylonian, Persian, Egyptian, and Greek thought can be detected in apocalyptic writings.[10]

Edlin also notes that ancient Israel's prophetic and apocalyptic literatures make use of symbolic language, give reports of visions, speak of end times, and predict God finally triumphing over evil. "In general," however, "prophetic literature tends to look for God's salvation within history, while apocalyptic literature sees God's salvation coming to fulfillment at the end of time."[11]

---

9. Tremper Longman III, *How to Read Daniel* (Downers Grove, IL: InterVarsity Press, 2020), 7-8, Kindle.
10. Edlin, *Daniel*, 22.
11. Ibid.

Apocalyptic Daniel and Prophetic Jeremiah

Tremper Longman III aptly illustrates the similarities and differences between the prophetic literature of Jeremiah and the apocalyptic literature of Daniel.[12]

1. Though God gave revelations to both men, each revelation had a different goal and thus led each individual to a different task.

2. God gave both Jeremiah and Daniel "a vision of the future." God spoke to Jeremiah directly with a message to give to God's people. The message was that they had broken "the covenant with God through their idolatry and other behaviors." Unless they repented, in their future God would bring punishment, including exile from their homeland. They did not repent, so at God's command, Jeremiah's message changed to one of coming judgment.[13]

3. In contrast, "God never speaks to Daniel directly." Rather, Daniel saw things and events in dreams and visions that he did not understand. It was a heavenly and angelic person (Gabriel), apparently sent from God, who comes and explains them. In contrast to Jeremiah, Daniel is not told to "share his revelation with the people." Daniel had no message for God's people asking them to repent. Rather, the written form of his book was a message of hope: a reassurance to the people that God was in control of world events and that those who oppressed God's people would be judged.[14]

4. Thus the prophets were often (though not always) "the bearers of bad news"—that is, judgment would come within history. Daniel was "the bearer of good news"—that is, God's final victory would come at the end of time.[15]

---

12. Longman, *How to Read Daniel*, 8-12.
13. Ibid., 8.
14. Ibid., 9.
15. Ibid.

The Literary Structure of the Book of Daniel

Whether you, the reader, view the book of Daniel to be the product of a narrator or one of Daniel's associates in the sixth century BC or see it as the work of an anonymous author or authors in the second century BC, the book as we now have it "stands as a well-designed unit of material."[16] That is, the stories of chapters 1–6 and the visions of chapters 7–12, when read continuously, "progress historically, from the earliest date to the latest. Common themes thread through each chapter and bind both parts of the book together."[17] The "earliest" date refers to Daniel 1:1, "the third year of the reign of Jehoiakim," which would be 605 BC, and the "latest" date refers to 10:1, "the third year of Cyrus," which would be 537-536 BC. The book, then, covers a span of sixty-nine years in the life of Daniel.

Scholars have suggested some rather creative analyses of the literary structure of the book of Daniel. The most straightforward approach, and possibly the one that readers most easily understand, however, is to view the book in its two most obvious divisions: *stories or court tales* (chs. 1–6) and *visions* (chs. 7–12). Still, there is a uniqueness to Daniel 7, since it functions as a "hinge" chapter between the two divisions. (See section titled "The Vision's Relationship, If Any, to the Other Three Visions or Previous Six Stories," in ch. 12, "Vision One [Dan. 7]," p. 149.)

An Outline of the Book of Daniel

An outline of the book of Daniel would look like the following:

I. Daniel 1–6: Stories of Daniel and His Friends Hananiah, Mishael, and Azariah at the Babylonian Court

A. *Story One (Dan. 1)*: Daniel and His Friends Refuse to Eat from King Nebuchadnezzar's Table; God Gave Them Knowledge and Understanding.

---

16. Edlin, *Daniel*, 31.
17. Ibid.

B. *Story Two (Dan. 2)*: The God of Heaven Revealed to Daniel King Nebuchadnezzar's Dream of an Enormous Statue and Its Interpretation.

C. *Story Three (Dan. 3)*: The Most High God Delivered Shadrach, Meshach, and Abednego from the Blazing Furnace.

D. *Story Four (Dan. 4)*: The Most High God Gave Daniel the Interpretation of King Nebuchadnezzar's Dream of an Enormous Tree.

E. *Story Five (Dan. 5)*: The Most High God Gave Daniel the Interpretation of the Handwriting on the Wall at King Belshazzar's Great Banquet.

F. *Story Six (Dan. 6)*: The Angel of the Living God Delivered Daniel from the Mouths of Lions in the Den.

II. Daniel 7–12: Daniel's Four Visions for the Future of God's People

A. *Vision One (Dan. 7)*: Daniel Saw Four Great Beasts, a Little Horn, the Ancient of Days, the One like a Son of Man.

B. *Vision Two (Dan. 8)*: Daniel Saw a Two-Horned Ram and a Shaggy Goat, Which Symbolized Media, Persia, and Greece.

C. *Vision Three (Dan. 9)*: Daniel Prayed a Prayer for Israel's Forgiveness; Gabriel Brought Him a Message from Heaven That Was Cast in a "Seventy 'Sevens'" Time Frame.

D. *Vision Four (Dan. 10–12)*: Daniel Saw a Revelation of a Future Great War.

3

Issues That Influence
Your Interpretation

When and Who?

The most essential issue that influences how you interpret the book of Daniel is your view of when it was written and who wrote it. Earlier, we discussed the traditional and the nontraditional views. Let's again consider these two views.

The *nontraditional view* understands the book of Daniel to have been produced in the second century BC by an anonymous author, writing in the name of a presumed legendary sixth-century BC prophet named Daniel. This view assumes there were fictional legends (the "court tales" [chs. 1–6]) about this Daniel, passed down through several centuries, to which this anonymous second-century BC author added messages (the visions [chs. 7–12]). These visions were of historical events that had *already* taken place. He presented them, however, as though they were prophecy from the legendary sixth-century Daniel. The supposed purpose of this combined book was to give hope to Jews living under Greek oppression in the second century BC. One of the main present-day proponents of this view is John Goldingay, who asserts that Daniel was written "in Jerusalem in the mid-160s BC" while

Antiochus Epiphanes IV was persecuting the Jews.[1] Goldingay later explains that the interpretation of Daniel is not dependent on its historicity or its time of authorship—"whether in the sixth century BC, the second, or somewhere in between." It does not matter if the visions are predictive prophecy or if the author was someone other than Daniel.[2]

As noted earlier, the *traditional view* understands the book of Daniel to have been written in the sixth century BC by a narrator who lived in Daniel's time or shortly after. This view understands "that the book presents authentic history in the stories and genuine prophecy in the visions."[3]

Moreover, the fact that the book of Daniel was deemed long ago by Jewish theologians to be Scripture, while other Jewish apocalyptic books were rejected as Scripture, speaks to the nature of the book of Daniel. It was deemed to be the Word of God right along with other sacred texts of Scripture. As the Word of God, then, the book of Daniel speaks truth to its readers. And it speaks truth not only in its theological content but also in its "first truth." "First truth" is when the text of the book states, for example, "Daniel then said to the guard . . ." (1:11), or "Then Daniel praised the God of heaven" (2:19), or "I, Daniel, understood from the Scriptures . . ." (9:2). What are readers of this text to believe? That the text is indeed telling this first truth, that it was indeed Daniel who "said," "praised," and "understood"? If the theological content of the book of Daniel is indeed the Word of God, then the "envelope" in which it is contained—the statements about who spoke those theological truths—is likewise the Word of God. The "envelope" itself is not fictional.

Does God Reveal Future Events?

At issue, too, is whether a person believes that God is capable of knowing future events and revealing them to his prophets so that they might

---

1. Goldingay, *Daniel*, 131.
2. Ibid., 134.
3. Edlin, *Daniel*, 36.

prophetically predict their happening. W. Sibley Towner is one scholar who speaks against this possibility. He says,

> We need to assume that the vision [of Daniel] as a whole is a prophecy after the fact. Why? Because human beings are unable accurately to predict future events centuries in advance and to say that Daniel could do so, even on the basis of a symbolic revelation vouchsafed to him by God and interpreted by an angel, is to fly in the face of the certainties of human nature. So what we have here is in fact not a road map of the future laid down in the sixth century B.C. but an interpretation of the events of the author's own time, 167-164 B.C.[4]

Tremper Longman III, unconvinced by Towner's argument, draws attention to the apostle Peter, who affirmed, "prophecy never had its origin in the human will, but prophets, though human, spoke from God as they were carried along by the Holy Spirit" (2 Pet. 1:21). Moreover, says Longman, "according to [the prophet] Isaiah, God's ability to know the future is precisely what differentiates him from false gods ([Isa.] 41:25-29; 42:8-9; 44:6-8)."[5]

Historical and Cultural Context

The stories and visions of the book of Daniel are set within specific ancient Middle Eastern cultural and historical settings. These settings are those of the Babylonians and Persians, who ruled the biblical world in succession throughout Daniel's lifetime. And even more specifically, the settings are those of the royal courts. We must, then, first read and interpret Daniel within those cultural and historical contexts with as much discernment as is possible from this great temporal and cultural distance.

---

4. W. Sibley Towner, *Daniel*, Interpretation: A Bible Commentary for Teaching and Preaching (Louisville, KY: Westminster John Knox, 2011), 115.

5. Longman, *How to Read Daniel*, 32.

Is the Book of Daniel Christian Scripture?

The book of Daniel is located securely in what Christians call the Old Testament. Yet it is part of *Christian* Scripture because for centuries Christians have viewed the *whole* Bible as Christian Scripture. Therefore, says Jim Edlin,

Daniel needs to be read in reference to the NT and Christian tradition. The ways in which both NT writers and Christian interpreters have understood and reapplied the message of the book should guide modern interpreters. The interpretations of the NT writers must bear added weight since they are not simply another opinion but inspired scripture.[6]

Was Daniel a Prophet?

In the Hebrew Bible (the Old Testament as it is arranged in the Hebrew language), Daniel is placed among the grouping known as the Writings, rather than among the grouping called the Prophets. The Writings, observes R. K. Harrison, was "reserved for the heterogeneous works of seers, wise men, and priests, or for those [works] that do not mention the name or work of a prophet."[7]

The Greek translation of the Old Testament (the Septuagint or LXX), however, placed the book of Daniel among the Prophets, following Ezekiel, an indication that the Jewish translators-organizers, who spoke Hebrew and Greek, viewed Daniel as one of Israel's major prophets, though in fact he was not called a prophet in the book itself.

An ascetic sect of Jews lived in the Judean Desert near the Wadi Qumran on the northwest edge of the Dead Sea from about 150 BC to about AD 68. Many manuscripts and fragments of biblical and non-biblical documents have been found in the vicinity of this site, most likely produced by this community of Jews. These documents are in the Hebrew, Aramaic, and Greek languages. One document, numbered 4Q174 by modern-day scholars,

---

6. Edlin, *Daniel*, 34.
7. R. K. Harrison, "Daniel, Book of," in *The International Standard Bible Encyclopedia*, ed. Geoffrey W. Bromiley (Grand Rapids: Eerdmans, 1979), 1:860.

written in Hebrew, is of special interest for our discussion here. In column four of this document, the unknown author wrote, "This is the [time of which] it is written in the book of Daniel the prophet" (the brackets in the quote are original).[8] He then follows this with partial quotes from Daniel 12:10 and 11:32.[9] Martin Abegg Jr. dates this document to about 25 BC, noting that the unknown author's comment cited above "suggests that at Qumran Daniel was included among the Prophets and not among the Writings."[10] A half-century or so after Qumran document 4Q174, Jesus Christ, while on the Mount of Olives teaching his disciples concerning "the end of the age," also made reference to "the prophet Daniel" (Matt. 24:3, 15).

So both the Qumran community and Jesus appear to have thought of Old Testament Daniel as a prophet.

The Overriding Theological Issue in the Book of Daniel: Is God Absolutely Sovereign?

Earthly kings do, indeed, hold sovereignty, for they rule over kingdoms and peoples. But their sovereignty is not an inherent sovereignty; it is a granted sovereignty, given to them by a power greater than themselves. Daniel affirmed this in a nighttime song of praise to the "God of heaven" when he chanted, "He deposes kings and raises up others" (Dan. 2:19, 21). In the New Testament, the apostle Paul stated a similar affirmation when he said, "There is no authority except that which God has established. The authorities that exist have been established by God" (Rom. 13:1).

All stories and visions in the book of Daniel stress this granted human sovereignty while highlighting the author's unalterable belief in the absolute sovereignty of the God of Israel over all things earthly and heavenly.

8. Michael Wise, Martin Abegg Jr., and Edward Cook, *The Dead Sea Scrolls: A New Translation* (San Francisco: HarperSanFrancisco, 1996), 228.

9. Ibid.

10. Martin Abegg Jr., Peter Flint, and Eugene Ulrich, *The Dead Sea Scrolls Bible: The Oldest Known Bible Translated for the First Time into English* (New York: HarperSanFrancisco, 1999), 484.

4

Chapter Summaries

The following summaries provide a helpful overview of the book of Daniel. In keeping with the structure of Daniel, chapters are classified as either stories or visions.

The First Story (Dan. 1)

Babylonian king Nebuchadnezzar ordered that Daniel and his three companions eat "food and wine from the king's table" (Dan. 1:5). They did not obey this order, though the story is narrated in such a way that it appears the king never knew of their disobedience. It was God who secretly thwarted the king's sovereignty. The author says, "God gave to Daniel favor and compassion before the chief of the officials" (v. 9, AT), and "To these four young men God gave knowledge and insight" (v. 17, AT).

The Second Story (Dan. 2)

Here, the despotic nature of King Nebuchadnezzar is revealed. He believed he held absolute sovereignty over the subjects of his kingdom. Jim Edlin describes him "as unreasonably demanding, unduly suspicious, and irrationally ruthless."[1] This plays out in the never-before-heard-of "game" he

---

1. Edlin, *Daniel*, 65.

attempted to play with his "magicians, enchanters, sorcerers and astrologers" (Dan. 2:2). In this "game" he demanded that they tell him *both* his dream of the previous night and its interpretation! But the sadistic joy he would have experienced at their inability to tell him the dream—which he would have derived from cutting them into pieces and reducing their houses to rubble—was thwarted by the "God of heaven" (vv. 18-19, 28, 37, 44) or the "great God" (v. 45). The outcome of this humiliating experience was that King Nebuchadnezzar declared to Daniel, "Truly, your God is God of gods and Lord of kings" (v. 47, ESV). This was at least a partial recognition of God's sovereignty (see the next story).

The Third Story (Dan. 3)

King Nebuchadnezzar still had not learned the limits of his perceived absolute earthly sovereignty. When "some Jews . . . Shadrach, Meshach and Abednego" refused to "serve [his] gods [or] worship the image of gold" that he had erected, he became furious and had them tossed "into the blazing furnace" (Dan. 3:12, 20).

Again, the "Most High God" thwarted King Nebuchadnezzar's sadistic act of sovereign power. When the king attempted to burn these three Jews alive, God preserved them in the midst of that fire. The text reads literally, "the fire did not rule [*lā' šĕlēṭ*] over their bodies" (AT)—that is, it had "no sovereignty over" them.[2] Moreover, "not a hair of their heads was singed, nor their cloaks scorched, nor even a smell of fire on them" (v. 27, AT).

Yet, even though King Nebuchadnezzar declared "praise" to the God of these three Jews (v. 28) and commanded that no one in his kingdom "say anything against" their God, he could not let go of his perceived personal absolute sovereignty: the penalty for violating *this* command was to be hacked into pieces and to have one's house smashed into rubble (v. 29).

---

2. Ibid., 100.

The Fourth Story (Dan. 4)

In King Nebuchadnezzar's final appearance in the book of Daniel, life is still all about *him*, though he tried to make it appear he was boasting about the God who had prevailed in the previous story. He spoke of "the miraculous signs and wonders that the Most High God has performed *for me*" (Dan. 4:2 [3:32 HB];[3] emphasis added). So his boasting was still focused on *himself*.

In this story, Daniel interpreted for Nebuchadnezzar a troubling dream. In his interpretation, Daniel warned him that he would be driven from his throne until he would "acknowledge that the Most High is sovereign over all kingdoms on earth and gives them to anyone he wishes" (4:25 [v. 22 HB]). Daniel then urged Nebuchadnezzar, "Renounce your sins by doing what is right, and your wickedness by being kind to the oppressed" (v. 27 [24 HB]).

Even a year later, the king's heart still had not turned from his sovereign pride. Viewing the city of Babylon, he bragged, "Is not this the great Babylon I have built as the royal residence, by my mighty power and for the glory of my majesty?" (v. 30 [27 HB]).

God thwarted Nebuchadnezzar's pride in his perceived sovereignty by humbling him to live with the animals of nature for a period of time (v. 33 [30 HB]). At the end of this time he praised "the Most High . . . [who] does as he pleases . . . [who is] the King of heaven, because everything he does is right and all his ways are just" (vv. 34-37 [31-34 HB]).

The Fifth Story (Dan. 5)

For seven years following King Nebuchadnezzar's death in 562 BC, three short-reigning kings ruled the Babylonian Empire. Then, in 556 BC, a fellow named Nabonidus and his son Belshazzar led a successful coup;

---

3. Bracketed references marked HB are from the Hebrew Bible, which sometimes has chapters and/or verses numbered differently from English versions.

together they ruled the empire for the next seventeen years.[4] The story in Daniel 5 occurred in 539 BC, in the final year of their joint reign.

As Daniel 5 opens, Nabonidus had been an absentee king for a decade, ruling the empire from his royal palace in the Arabian Desert southeast of Edom, leaving son Belshazzar in charge of royal affairs in Babylon.[5] Belshazzar, apparently believing himself to be of some importance, was in the midst of giving a great feast. This was a lavish affair as evidenced by the one thousand important people invited to attend from all over the empire. His gaggle of wives and concubines was also present (vv. 1-2).

To show off his arrogance and "blatant blasphemy of Israel's God,"[6] Belshazzar ordered that the sacred gold and silver vessels that Nebuchadnezzar had stolen from Jerusalem's temple some six decades earlier be brought to the banquet hall to be used for drinking (v. 2). Why? Edlin suggests that "Drinking from the goblets . . . portrays blatant blasphemy of Israel's God."[7] Tanner says, "Belshazzar was not simply making an innocent mistake. Rather, he was knowingly and openly defying the Most High God."[8]

Daniel's confrontation of Belshazzar at the feast will be discussed in more detail later in this book. For now it is enough to observe that Daniel, in the presence of the entire assemblage of guests, boldly pointed out Belshazzar's pride. He declared, "And you . . . , Belshazzar, have not humbled your heart, . . . but you have lifted up yourself against the Lord of heaven" (vv. 22-23, ESV). It was pride—a belief in his own royal sovereignty—that led Belshazzar to believe that he and his guests could drink with impunity from the sacred vessels of the Jerusalem temple. In doing so, declared Daniel, "the God in whose hand is your breath, and whose are all your ways, you have not honored" (v. 23, ESV).

---

4. Bright, *History of Israel*, 352-53; Edlin, *Daniel*, 127-28.

5. Bright, *History of Israel*, 353.

6. Edlin, *Daniel*, 130.

7. Ibid.

8. J. Paul Tanner, *Daniel*, Evangelical Exegetical Commentary, ed. William D. Barrick (Bellingham, WA: Lexham Press, 2020), 326, Logos Bible Software.

The author concluded this story with these words: "That very night Belshazzar, king of the Babylonians, was slain, and Darius the Mede took over the kingdom, at the age of sixty-two" (vv. 30-31 [5:30–6:1 HB]). In this, he illustrated Daniel's earlier words: "The Most High God is sovereign over all kingdoms on earth and sets over them anyone he wishes" (5:21).

The Sixth Story (Dan. 6)

Thus, in one night, the rule of the empire changed hands. It was now ruled by one called Darius the Mede (see the sidebar "Who Was Darius the Mede?" below).

Who Was Darius the Mede?

Non-biblical documents do not know of a person by the name Darius the Mede. In the documents a Persian named Cyrus is the one who conquered Babylon in 539 BC. This Cyrus is known in later history as Cyrus the Great.

Modern scholars who view the date and authorship of the book of Daniel from a nontraditional viewpoint (second century BC) suggest that the author's knowledge of history was faulty and thus named a nonexistent conqueror of Babylon. Those who view the book from a traditional viewpoint (sixth century BC), however, and who desire to preserve the integrity of the book and its author's divine inspiration, look for clues within the text itself for a possible explanation. Jim Edlin suggests that such a clue may exist in Daniel 6:28 (v. 29 HB).[9]

The New International Version of Daniel 6:28 (v. 29 HB) reads, "So Daniel prospered during the reign of Darius and the reign of Cyrus the Persian." The "and" in this verse is the Aramaic *waw* and could grammatically be read as an explicative conjunctive (see the sidebar "The Explicative Conjunctive" on the following page). This verse, then, could be read, "So Daniel prospered during the reign of Darius, that is [*waw*], the reign of Cyrus the Persian." In support of this, ancient tradition understands

---

9. Edlin, *Daniel*, 148.

Cyrus's mother to have been the daughter of a Median king, while his father Cambyses was a royal Persian. Thus it is possible that Cyrus the Great carried two titles: Darius (Median) and Cyrus (Persian).[10]

The Explicative Conjunctive

Both Aramaic and Hebrew use a one-syllable conjunction that, in English transliteration, is spelled *waw* (but pronounced *vahv*); *waw* is basically equivalent in meaning to the English conjunction "and." *Waw*, however, also carries a number of other nuances or usages, one of which is called an explicative conjunctive.

An explicative conjunctive is a conjunction that joins two *phrases*, with the second phrase giving further explanation to the first.[11] English uses words other than "and" for an explicative conjunctive, such as "that is" or "even."

In this sixth story in the book of Daniel, human pride or a sense of royal sovereignty is not so prominent as in the previous stories involving Nebuchadnezzar and Belshazzar. Yet King Darius allowed pride to potentially cause the death of Daniel, one of his distinguished administrators, one who had showed "exceptional qualities . . . in his conduct of government affairs" (Dan. 6:3-4 [vv. 4-5 HB]).

The story of this nefarious affair will be discussed more fully later in this book. For now, it is enough to note that King Darius, because of apparent pride in his status as king, allowed himself to be duped or trapped by a group of unscrupulous "administrators and satraps" (v. 6 [7 HB]) into signing a premeditated edict, aimed at the murder of one person only—"Daniel, . . . one of the exiles from Judah" (v. 13 [14 HB]). This edict provided "that anyone

---

10. Ibid.

11. For the Aramaic and Hebrew use of the explicative conjunctive, see Bruce K. Waltke and M. O'Connor, *An Introduction to Biblical Hebrew Syntax* (Winona Lake, IN: Eisenbrauns, 1990), 39.2.1.b; and W. Gesenius, E. Kautzsch, and A. E. Cowley, *Gesenius' Hebrew Grammar*, 2nd ed., trans. A. E. Cowley (Oxford, UK: The Clarendon Press, 1910), sec. 154aN1*b*.

who prays to any god or human being during the next thirty days, except to you, Your Majesty, shall be thrown into the lions' den" (v. 7 [8 HB]).

Daniel refused to obey this edict, continuing to pray "three times a day . . . to his God" (v. 10 [11 HB]), resulting in his arrest and being tossed overnight into the lions' den (v. 16 [17 HB]).

The outcome of this whole nefarious affair was that God, whom King Darius acknowledged to be the "living God" (v. 20 [21 HB]), sent one whom Daniel said was God's "angel" to "shut the mouths of the lions" (v. 22 [23 HB]).

In the conclusion of this story, this earthly king of the largest empire the biblical world had ever known rejoiced that his very capable administrator Daniel was rescued from death. In this context, the king acknowledged the absolute sovereignty of God: the "living God" is eternal and the realm of his rulership extends to both "the heavens and on the earth" (vv. 26-27 [27-28 HB]).

Daniel's First Vision (Dan. 7)

This vision backtracks in time to "the first year of Belshazzar king of Babylon" (7:1), the year in which Daniel received the vision. This was about 550 BC when Nabonidus turned over to Belshazzar the running of the day-to-day matters of the empire from Babylon. He himself went off to his retreat center in the Arabian Desert.[12] Tremper Longman III observes that the vision then takes the reader "to the end of history."[13]

This vision was given to Daniel in a dream (v. 1). In verses 1-8, Daniel was beside the shore of a sea from which four beasts arose. From the fourth beast there came a figure in the form of a "horn, a little one, . . . that spoke boastfully" (v. 8). We learn later in the vision that its boastful speaking was "against the Most High" (v. 25).

In verses 9-14, Daniel was witness to a heavenly courtroom. There, seated upon a throne, was a figure called the "Ancient of Days," indicating God himself (v. 9). Tremper Longman III interprets this as "a title that indicates

12. Edlin, *Daniel*, 170.
13. Longman, *How to Read Daniel*, 97.

a person of great antiquity."[14] When the court officials had taken their seats, and the thousands of other attendants summoned as witnesses were in their places, "the books were opened" (v. 10).

Then, as though all preparations up to this point were for what now was to happen, into the presence of the Ancient of Days was brought "one like a son of man" (v. 13). Though his identity is not given in this vision, later New Testament writers and Christian interpreters have understood this figure to be Jesus Christ.

The purpose of the court session was to pass judgment on the four beasts and the little horn, to strip them of all earthly authority (vv. 11-12). This was done, and all "authority, glory and sovereign power" was then given to the "one like a son of man" whose "dominion" would be "an everlasting dominion" (vv. 13-14).

This handover of the "sovereignty, power and greatness of all the kingdoms under heaven" is restated to Daniel at the conclusion of this first vision (v. 27). It is to the "Most High" that all "will be handed over," to "an everlasting kingdom" in which God's "holy people" will have full participation (vv. 26-27).

Daniel's Second Vision (Dan. 8)

The timing of this vision is significant. It occurred "in the third year of King Belshazzar's reign" (8:1), which would be about 548 BC (his first year being about 550 BC). The significance is that, to the east of Babylon, Persian Cyrus was gaining power militarily. This was a harbinger of Babylon's coming downfall in less than a decade, when Cyrus would conquer Babylon in 539 BC.[15]

There is significance also in the location of Daniel's second vision: "Susa in the province of Elam" (v. 2). Most likely Daniel was not physically in Susa

---

14. Ibid., 100.
15. Tanner, *Daniel*, 485.

but "present there in visionary experience only."[16] Elam, with its city of Susa, was located eastward from Babylon in what later became known as Persia. The Persian king Darius I, who came to the Babylonian throne in 522 BC (second after Cyrus), moved his administrative capital to Susa. He militarily expanded the empire eastward to the doorstep of India, capturing the Indus Valley, and westward to the approaches to Greece, creating the largest land empire the world had ever known.

The details of this vision will be discussed later in this book. For now, the essence of this vision is that Daniel saw two symbolic animals. The first was a very powerful two-horned ram, one horn short, the other long. This ram seemed to be more powerful than any other animal (vv. 3-4).

The second was a powerful one-horned goat that came out of the west and rammed the ram, shattering both its horns (vv. 5-7). This goat, in turn, became great, until another power broke off *its* horn. In the place of that one horn, however, there came up four horns, representing four powers. Out of one of these four new horns-powers came a small horn that became increasingly powerful, expanding into the "Beautiful Land" (v. 9), a term for Judah and/or Jerusalem. This small horn, believing itself to be all-powerful, set itself against the "Prince of the host" (v. 11, ESV, NKJV). In this context, the "Prince" is God himself. The "host" refers to both heavenly beings (v. 10) and the "LORD's people" (vv. 12-13; see also v. 24) who worship him in the Jerusalem temple.[17] This little horn-power violated the "daily sacrifice" in the Jerusalem "sanctuary" (or "temple") and trampled "truth" underfoot (vv. 11-12). Its power seemed invincible.

In this second vision, the angel Gabriel came and interpreted the main points of the vision for Daniel: the two-horned ram represented the Empire of Media and Persia, and the goat represented the Empire of Greece. The little horn-power "will consider himself superior. . . . He will . . . take his stand

---

16. Lucas, *Daniel*, 204.
17. Edlin, *Daniel*, 200-201.

against the Prince of princes. Yet he will be destroyed, but not by human power" (v. 25).

The ultimate message of this second vision to Daniel is that in the course of human history that will continue centuries beyond his own time, even to the "time of the end" (v. 17), God is sovereign over all earthly kingdoms and all rulers.

Daniel's Third Vision (Dan. 9)

The time reference for Daniel's experience recorded in Dan 9 is the "first year of Darius . . . a Mede" (v. 1). This person appears to be the same Darius-Cyrus who conquered Babylon in 539 BC (see the sidebar "Who Was Darius the Mede?" in section titled "The Sixth Story [Dan. 6]," p. 32). The author does not give Daniel's location at this time.

This third vision report consists of two major parts. *The first part, 9:3-19,* reports Daniel's prayer of confession on behalf of his people. In verse 3, Daniel said he addressed his prayer to the "Lord God." Here, "Lord" (lowercase letters) represents the Hebrew word *'ădōnāy,* or "Adonay." When this term is used in direct address to God, it is a *title* meaning "Sovereign." So Daniel addressed his prayer to God as "Sovereign God." God as Sovereign, his rule over all, then, is the immediate focus of this vision.

Then, in v. 4*a,* Daniel said he "prayed to the LORD." Here, "LORD" (uppercase letters) represents the Hebrew word *yhwh,* or "Yahweh." The author of the Genesis creation account introduced the compound "LORD God [*yhwh 'ĕlōhîm*]" in Genesis 2:4 "for the purpose of identifying *Yahweh* as the God who creates (as opposed to Marduk, Ptah, or others)."[18] He is the creator of all that exists in "the earth and the heavens" (v. 4). This is the *name* by which God later made himself known to Moses and by which he said he was to be called throughout all succeeding generations of Israelites (Exod. 3:15).

---

18. Joseph Colson, *Genesis 1–11,* New Beacon Bible Commentary (Kansas City: Beacon Hill Press of Kansas City, 2012), 83.

In Daniel 9:4*b*, in his prayer itself, Daniel addressed God as "Lord" (Adonay-Sovereign). At stake is whether or not Sovereign Yahweh will continue his covenant relationship with the people of Judah, Jerusalem, and Israel (v. 7).

Daniel opened his prayer with, "Please, O Lord-Sovereign . . . Keeper of covenant and fidelity [NIV: "love"; ESV and NRSV: "steadfast love"] with lovers of him and with keepers of his commandments" (v. 4, AT). "Covenant" and "keeping" were the controlling features of this relationship. Sovereign is faithful, but, alas, confessed Daniel, we are not: "We have . . . done wrong . . . been wicked . . . rebelled . . . turned away . . . not listened . . . not obeyed" (vv. 5-6, 14). Therefore, Daniel admitted, the scattering of your people throughout countries hither and yon (v. 7) and the devastation of Jerusalem (v. 12) are justly deserved.

Is there a future hope of restoration for God's people? Is their punishment to be forever? But because God is Sovereign-Adonay, he can *choose* to "look with favor" (v. 17). Daniel is banking on this single fact—that it is "because of your great mercy" that Sovereign-Adonay will "forgive" (vv. 18-19).

In *the second part, 9:20-27*, the angel Gabriel showed up from heaven with a message while Daniel was still in the act of praying and confessing (vv. 20-21). The purpose of his coming, Gabriel said, was that Daniel might "consider the word and understand the vision" (v. 23). The "word" might refer to the "word of the LORD given to Jeremiah" mentioned in verse 2, while the "vision" is what Daniel is about to receive.[19]

The main essence of Gabriel's message was that God's people would experience a period of great suffering, during which there would be destruction in their beloved Jerusalem and the desecration of their temple sanctuary (v. 26). Yet God would bring about an end to this (vv. 26-27), for he "remains sovereign over all that happens and orchestrates his final plan as he sees fit."[20]

---

19. Edlin, *Daniel*, 227.
20. Ibid., 240.

Daniel's Fourth Vision (Dan. 10–12)

The time reference given for Daniel's vision recorded in Daniel 10:1–12:13 is the "third year of Cyrus king of Persia" (10:1). This would be 537-536 BC. In this vision Daniel engaged in a dialogue with a figure whom Daniel described as "a man" (v. 5), who apparently is a messenger from heaven. From Daniel's rather dazzling description (vv. 5-6), this messenger was surely at least an angel. Stephen Miller even suggests that this person may have been God himself "because of the overwhelming effect of his presence on Daniel" (see vv. 8-9) or perhaps even the preincarnate Christ because of the close "parallel to the portrait of Christ in Rev. 1:12-16."[21]

This fourth vision may be viewed in three divisions.[22] *Division one* (Dan. 10:1–11:1) is the *setting* of the vision. It consists of this heavenly messenger giving Daniel details of his journey through the spiritual realm when coming to him. He also prepared Daniel through words of encouragement to receive the message of the vision.

Division two (11:1–12:4) is the *message* of Daniel's fourth vision. Jim Edlin calls this "a prophetic survey" of the history of the Persian and Greek Empires, beginning with events from the reign of Persian Cyrus the Great, which began in 556 BC, through the rule of Greek Antiochus IV, which ended in 164 BC.[23]

It is from 11:21 on that this fourth vision describes historical events during the reign of Greek Antiochus IV (175-164 BC). He is described as "a contemptible person" (v. 21), one who acts "deceitfully" (v. 23), one who is "against the holy covenant" (v. 30), one who will "desecrate the temple" (v. 31) and will speak "against the God of gods" (v. 36). "He will extend his power over many countries" (v. 42). "Yet," says the vision, "he will come to his end, and no one will help him" (v. 45).

---

21. Miller, *Daniel*, n.p.
22. Edlin, *Daniel*, 240.
23. Ibid., 252-54.

Division three (12:5-13) is a word of *assurance* to Daniel: "At the end of the days you will rise" (v. 13). This is a promise of resurrection, not only for Daniel but also for "everyone whose name is found written in the book . . . [for] those who are wise" (vv. 1, 3).

The ultimate message is, "Hang in there! God is sovereign!" In the end, not only will God triumph, but so will "the people who know their God . . . those who are wise" (11:32-33). The promise to Daniel of resurrection from "rest" (12:13)—"rest" here meaning death—is not just a tacked-on promise unrelated to the vision. It is God's promise of his final sovereignty over earth's humans who cause death to his people. "Death will not hold you, Daniel. You will live again." Here is the Old Testament's clearest affirmation concerning belief in personal resurrection.[24] In the New Testament, Paul (rephrasing Hosea's hint at resurrection in Hos. 13:14) declared that the fullness of resurrection has already been accomplished for all "through our Lord Jesus Christ" (1 Cor. 15:57).

---

24. Lucas, *Daniel*, 302.

5

How to Read and Interpret
the Book of Daniel

Read the *Entire Book*

You, the reader of the book of Daniel, will highly benefit from reading the entire book in one sitting, if possible, before attempting to interpret in depth each chapter (story or vision) separately. By reading the book in its entirety, though you will not remember all its data, you will have the larger picture into which to fit the smaller pieces and units as you proceed.

Chapters 1–6: The Stories

Retelling Each Story

In part II of this book, I will retell the story contained in each of chapters 1–6 in *my* own words. This may not be the way you would retell the story, however. So you will retain the essence of each story much better if you also take time to retell it to someone else in *your* words.

Customs and Practices Explained

The author of these six stories includes references to some ancient Middle Eastern customs and practices, which he assumes his readers understand without need for explanation. These are quite unfamiliar to us in our present-day world, however. I will note these and give insights into their meanings, at least what scholars say from their research into ancient documents. You may also want to search in Bible dictionaries, Bible encyclopedias, and books on Bible backgrounds for further tidbits of information.

God behind the Scenes

With each of the six stories, I will attempt to bring to the fore the author's hints that he is telling an intertwined story. That is, the author is not merely telling a story of humans interacting with humans. Rather, in *all* instances there is another person or power acting behind, and sometimes within, the scenes of history that influences the outcome. That person or power, the author is convinced, is the God of Israel.

The Story's Relationship, If Any, to the Other Five Stories or Four Visions

These six stories are not independent of each other. Each is related in some way to what has been told before and to what is told after. I will note how these stories are interconnected, how a theme of one story may be repeated in another and/or others, and how the author may be presenting a unified theme in all six stories.

Faithful Living Today

To read, understand the content, and interpret the meaning of a biblical book is a worthy academic exercise. But when all is said and done, if a person has not gained any insight from this exercise that impacts his or her life and lifestyle, it remains only that—an exercise. Therefore, I will make suggestions for our faithful living today. What might the stories of the faithfulness of these ancient sixth-century BC Israelite servants of the living God, living under the oppressiveness of foreign, non-God-fearing rulers, have to say to Christians living in the twenty-first century AD?

Chapters 7–12: The Visions

Retell Each Vision in Your Own Words

In part II of this book, I will retell the vision of each of the four visions of chapters 7–12 in *my* own words, but this may not be the way you would retell the vision. So you will retain the essence of each vision much better if you also retell it in *your* words.

Idioms, Concepts, and Ancient Beliefs

The ancients' use of certain idiomatic expressions, their symbolic use of numbers, and concepts of the connectedness of heavenly and earthly powers are examples of some things that need explanation. I will attempt to explain these matters insofar as present-day scholars and researchers understand such things. Again, you may want to research further by consulting Bible dictionaries, Bible encyclopedias, and books on Bible backgrounds for further tidbits of information.

The Vision's Relationship, If Any, to the Other Three Visions or Previous Six Stories

These four visions are not independent of each other. Each in some way relates to the others and even to the stories that precede them. I will note these relationships, if any, and highlight the significance of that (inter)relationship.

Faithful Living

From the visions of chapters 7–12, I will suggest insights for faithful living that God's people may appropriate for living in the twenty-first century AD.

PART II

INTERPRETING THE BOOK OF DANIEL

6

Story One (Dan. 1)

Summary

The first story is aptly summarized as follows: (1) Daniel and his friends declined to eat food and drink wine assigned to them from the king's kitchen (Dan. 1:8). (2) *God* gave them knowledge and understanding (v. 17).

The Story

The story of Daniel begins with a reference to Babylon's king Nebuchadnezzar and his army invading the kingdom of Judah and aggressively moving against Judah's capital city, Jerusalem. This happened early in the reign of Judah's king Jehoiakim, sometime between 604 and 601 BC (1:1).[1] Elsewhere, two other biblical historians describe King Jehoiakim as one who was prone to doing evil in the sight of the "LORD [Yahweh]" (2 Kings 23:37; 2 Chron. 36:5). The author of Daniel does not comment on King Jehoiakim's evilness, but perhaps his view is subtly revealed in his statement "The Lord ["Adonay" or "Sovereign"] gave Jehoiakim king of Judah into his [i.e., Nebuchadnezzar's] hand, with some of the vessels of the house of God" (Dan. 1:2, ESV). Jim Edlin comments: "The circumstances behind the story of Dan

---

1. Lucas, *Daniel*, 51.

47

1 did not take place by accident. . . . God had orchestrated these events. Jerusalem was given into the hands of Nebuchadnezzar as an act of divine judgment."[2]

Thus King Jehoiakim was powerless to prevent King Nebuchadnezzar from breaking into Jerusalem. His confiscation of the temple vessels was intended to show that in allowing him to defeat the Judeans, his gods were more powerful than the God of the Judeans. So he took the Jerusalem temple vessels to Babylon and put them for safekeeping in the temple treasury of his gods (v. 2). But, observes John Goldingay, these temple vessels did not, in fact, belong to Nebuchadnezzar's Babylonian gods, as if they, by their power, had won them. It was *God* who had handed them over to Nebuchadnezzar. It is Judah's God who is in control.[3] In fact, these sacred vessels would now be safely in storage in Babylon. (Of these sacred vessels, the "gold and silver goblets" will surface later in story five, when Babylonian king Belshazzar has them brought from storage so that he and his guests may drink from them at a great royal banquet [see 5:1-3].)

The author of the Daniel story uses his reference to King Nebuchadnezzar's "god in Babylonia" to transition his story from Jerusalem to "Babylonia" (1:2).

The Vessels of the Jerusalem Temple

It probably would have been the smaller vessels of gold, silver, and bronze in the Jerusalem temple that Solomon had made. These smaller vessels would have been more easily carried away by King Nebuchadnezzar to Babylon and "put in the treasure house of his god" (Dan. 1:2). Many of these are noted in 2 Chronicles 4: "a hundred gold sprinkling bowls" (v. 8), "pots and shovels and [other] sprinkling bowls" (v. 11), "meat forks" (v. 16), "tongs [of] . . . solid gold" (v. 21), and "pure gold wick trimmers, sprinkling bowls, dishes and censers" (v. 22). Note that Solomon had originally also "placed them in the treasuries of God's temple" (5:1).

---

2. Edlin, *Daniel*, 50.
3. Goldingay, *Daniel*, 163.

Those vessels that Nebuchadnezzar carried away to Babylon during King Jehoiakim's reign would be spared the destruction that would occur to the remaining vessels a few years later. During the reign of King Jehoiachin, Jehoiakim's successor, Nebuchadnezzar again came against Jerusalem, removed and cut into pieces all the remaining vessels of gold in the temple, and carried them away (2 Kings 24:13). Then, a few years later, during the reign of King Zedekiah, Jehoiachin's successor, Nebuchadnezzar again besieged Jerusalem, destroyed its walls and buildings, and burned the "temple of the LORD" (25:1-10).

The story now jumps right into tales of Daniel and his three friends—Hananiah, Mishael, and Azariah—and their life under royal captivity in Babylon. These four young men were among "the Israelites from the royal family and the nobility" mentioned in Daniel 1:3, though we are told nothing of their noble birth or lineage. We assume that they got caught up in Nebuchadnezzar's sweep of young men and women—Israelites and others—whom he took from the cities and towns that his army overran in his military campaigns to the west during the years 605-601 BC. These conscripts would have had no choice in the matter; they did not travel to Babylon for a vacation or on a sightseeing trip!

We are right away introduced to one of Nebuchadnezzar's court officials, named Ashpenaz. This fellow was no lower-rung-of-the-ladder employee, but rather "*chief* of his court officials" (v. 3; emphasis added).

Ashpenaz, himself, must have been an astute person, possessing a unique ability to judge human character and abilities. The king gave him an assignment in which he was to select several of the young male Israelite conscripts. They were to have no "physical defect" and were to be "handsome" (v. 4). This would not take any special astuteness; a person could observe such qualities with the physical eyes. But the other qualifications would require rather acute discernment: these must be men who "were skillful in all wisdom, knowing knowledge, understanding/perceiving knowledge, and in whom

was strength to stand/serve in the king's palace" (v. 4, AT). Moreover, after
selection, Ashpenaz "was to teach them the literature and language of the
Chaldeans [i.e., the Babylonians]" (v. 4, AT). This education process was to
continue over a period of three years (v. 5).

The author continues with, "And there were among them some Judeans"
(v. 6, AT), implying that this particular cohort to be trained for three years
consisted of more than Daniel, Hananiah, Mishael, and Azariah (whose
names were changed respectively to Belteshazzar, Shadrach, Meshach, and
Abednego). The others may have been "Babylonians and other foreigners."[4]
Surely, then, there would have been other Babylonian teachers assisting Ashpenaz in the training of this cohort of conscripts. All these teachers would
have been well versed and thoroughly trained in the arts, languages, and
literatures of Babylon. They were not slouches!

One aspect of the training regime of this cohort that created an issue for
Daniel and his three friends was their daily assignment of "food and wine
from the king's table" (v. 5). For a reason not revealed in the text, Daniel
"resolved not to defile himself with the royal food and wine" (v. 8), a resolution that included Hananiah, Mishael, and Azariah (v. 11).

Scholars have suggested several possible biblical explanations why Daniel considered eating and drinking this "royal food and wine" would be a
defilement. John Goldingay has examined several of the suggestions and has
convincingly shown them not to be biblically supported. These suggestions
include the following: the king's food might have first been offered to an idol
at the temple; the laws of the Torah concerning which animals and how to
kill and cook them would not be followed in the king's kitchen; one would
abstain from meat and wine, which are often festal foods, to indicate mourning; and one would abstain from meat and wine in preparation for receiving a divine revelation.[5] In their place, Goldingay suggests that eating and
drinking, among other activities, are external displays of self-identity and

---

4. Ibid., 157.
5. Ibid., 158-59.

that this is especially important for the exiled or persecuted. For Daniel and his friends, abstaining from the "royal food and wine" (v. 8) is a symbolic way of preserving their identity.[6]

Jim Edlin agrees but notes that challenging the food the king had prescribed was "a perilous" action "for a trainee." He suggests further that "Daniel the Israelite chose to distinguish himself from Babylonian values and beliefs. Yahweh's hero stood against Marduk's world."[7] Marduk was King Nebuchadnezzar's chief god, the patron deity of the city of Babylon.

Daniel's resolution not to eat and drink the king's provisions gave Ashpenaz, the chief official, some real anxiety. Surely, he laments, *they* would suffer physically if they did not eat such choice food and drink—they would appear less healthy than other trainees in the cohort, wouldn't they! Even more, he himself, *Ashpenaz*, might even lose his own head! (v. 10).

So Daniel graciously backed off from negotiating with Ashpenaz. He turned to a lower-rung official, whom the New International Version identifies as "the guard" (vv. 11, 16; see the sidebar "'The Guard' and the Meaning of Cognate" below).

This points to a well-organized system for the three-year educational process of court trainees. Depending on the number in this particular cohort of trainees, there might be several lower-rung overseers for groups of four or five each. It seems that Ashpenaz had delegated the food-and-drink responsibility for these four Israelites to this overseer (v. 11).

"The Guard" and the Meaning of Cognate

"The guard" (Dan. 1:11) is the New International Version's translation of the Hebrew term *hammelṣar*, which appears to be a loanword from Akkadian, thus a cognate of the Akkadian word *maṣṣaru/massartu*. In Akkadian, the word means "watcher," "supervisor."[8]

---

6. Ibid., 159.
7. Edlin, *Daniel*, 56.
8. Shalom M. Paul, "The Mesopotamian Babylonian Background of Daniel 1–6," in *The Book of Daniel: Composition and Reception*, ed. John J. Collins and Peter W. Flint (Leiden, NL: Brill, 2001), 1:62; *The Assyrian*

Cognate signifies a word in two or more languages with the same meaning and from the same original root but with the spelling usually somewhat different, such as English "is," German *ist*, Latin *est*, originally from Indo-European *esti*.

Daniel's request of the overseer was for a simple test lasting only ten days. Using proper language when addressing a superior—he referred to the four of them as "your servants"—he asked that they be permitted to eat only vegetables and drink only water (v. 12). Then, at the end of the ten days, their appearance should be compared with others in the cohort who ate and drank the allotment of the "royal food" (v. 13). The overseer agreed to the test. At the end of the ten days, the four Israelite young men appeared in so much better physical shape than the others in the cohort that for the remainder of their three-year training, the overseer gave them a permanent pass on the food provision from the king's larder (vv. 12-16).

The author now coalesces the four young men's three-year training into just two sentences: "And these four young men! God gave to them knowledge and insight in all literature and wisdom. And Daniel! He was perceptive in every kind of vision and dream" (v. 17, AT).

The irony in this tale is that for three years King Nebuchadnezzar was under the delusion that he was in charge, that his orders were being obeyed. The humor here is that this king, who believes himself to have absolute sovereignty over all his subjects and conscripts, is being undermined right within his own palace precincts.

So at the conclusion of the cohort's three-year training, Ashpenaz (the "chief official" [v. 18]) reenters the story. It was he who presented the four Israelite young men to King Nebuchadnezzar. The king examined Daniel, Hananiah, Mishael, and Azariah concerning matters that would require

---

Dictionary of the Oriental Institute of the University of Chicago (Chicago: Oriental Institute, 1977), vol. 10M, pt. 1: 333-34, 341-42.

"perceptive wisdom" (v. 20, AT). They passed their exams with flying colors! In fact, if the king had been giving letter grades, they each would have received an A+ and have been awarded right then membership in the Honor Society of Babylonian Magicians. Their exam grade was declared to be "ten times better than all the magicians and enchanters in [the king's] whole kingdom" (v. 20). Thus, concludes the author, "they entered the king's service" (v. 19). Goldingay observes, "The Israelite kingly family has been taken into the service of the Babylonian king."[9]

These magicians and enchanters, introduced here as offstage characters, will come to the foreground in later stories in full enmity against these four Israelite men!

Customs and Practices Explained

Articles from the Jerusalem Temple (Dan. 1:2)

The author reports that King Nebuchadnezzar confiscated "some of the articles from the temple of God" in Jerusalem. He carried them away and put them into the "treasure house of his god" in Babylon. Kings in the ancient biblical world fought wars in the names of their gods. Therefore, any booty captured belonged to those gods. Carrying off the idols of a conquered people signified that the conquering king's god was more powerful than the god or gods of the conquered people. Since the Judeans had no idols in their temple, the articles and utensils used in the acts of worship took the place of idols. Confiscating them indicated that Nebuchadnezzar believed his god, Marduk, was more powerful than Judah's God, Yahweh.

The Land of Shinar (Dan. 1:2)

The New International Version says that Nebuchadnezzar put the articles from the Jerusalem temple in the "temple of his god in Babylonia." The Hebrew for "Babylonia" is literally "land of Shinar," a term for this land even

---

9. Goldingay, *Daniel*, 171.

more ancient than the time of Daniel. In Genesis 10:10, for example, it refers to the larger area in which the city of Babylon and other cities of mighty Nimrod's kingdom were located. Genesis 11:1-9 identifies the land of "Shinar" (v. 2) as the area in which humanity, in rebellion against God's command to fill the earth, was attempting to build the city of Babel and remain settled (v. 9). In Zechariah 5:5-11, the prophet Zechariah saw in a vision two winged creatures flying "between heaven and earth" (v. 9) with a basket filled with the wickedness of God's people. When he asked an interpreting angel where they were taking the basket, he said, "To the land of Shinar" (v. 11, AT [NIV: "Babylonia"]). Thomas McComiskey comments that "in the prophetic books Shinar represents oppressing nations." Thus these winged creatures are "removing Wickedness to an appropriate place, that is, to where idolatry, oppression, and cruelty already abide."[10] Goldingay summarizes, "In the OT, the name especially suggests a place of false religion, self-will, and self-aggrandizement."[11]

Deportation of Royalty (Dan. 1:3)

The author mentions "some of the Israelites from the royal family and the nobility." This is just a hint of what the Babylonian kings (and others before them) practiced upon conquering a city or kingdom. On the one hand, negatively, deporting members of the royal family and others of noble status would weaken that city's or kingdom's ability to mount rebellion in the future. On the other hand, positively, the Babylonian king is to be credited with wisdom in recognizing that his empire would significantly benefit from incorporating into its various levels of leadership those "foreigners" of high intellectual abilities. As time passed, they would become good "Babylonians."

---

10. Thomas E. McComiskey, ed., *Zephaniah, Haggai, Zechariah, and Malachi*, vol. 3 of *The Minor Prophets: An Exegetical and Expository Commentary* (Grand Rapids: Baker, 1998), 1103.

11. Goldingay, *Daniel*, 154.

The Kasdim (Dan. 1:4)

In this verse occurs the phrase "the language and literature of the Babylonians." In the Hebrew text, however, the term that the New International Version translates "Babylonians" is *Kasdim* (*im* is a Hebrew plural ending; thus Goldingay calls them "Kasdites"[12]). The *Kasdim* were a people from southern Mesopotamia from which Nebuchadnezzar's father, Nabopolassar, came. In 626, Nabopolassar took control of Babylon, and his family continued to rule until Persian Cyrus came to Babylonian power in 539 BC. Thus *Kasdim* refers to the ruling class in Babylonia for over a century. The term occurs with this meaning three times in Daniel (1:4; 5:30; 9:1).

Kasdim, however, is also used in Daniel eight times for a class of Babylonian scholars, which the New International Version translates as "astrologers" (2:2, 4-5, 10; 3:8; 4:7 [v. 4 HB]; 5:7, 11). The common spoken and written language of Babylonia at the time of Daniel, and used internationally, was Aramaic, a language similar to Hebrew. The language of Babylonian scholarly, historical, and sacred texts, however, was Akkadian. To be among the *Kasdim*, a person must read and write this language, and to do this, a person must become skilled in cuneiform, a very complicated system of writing. John Goldingay summarizes the role of the *Kasdim*:

> They were the guardians of the sacred traditional lore developed and preserved in Mesopotamia over centuries, covering natural history, astronomy, mathematics, medicine, myth, and chronicle. Much of this learning had a practical purpose, being designed to be applied to life by means of astrology, oneirology, hepatoscopy and the study of other organs, rites of purification, sacrifice, incantation, exorcism and other forms of divination.[13]

---

12. Ibid., 155.
13. Ibid.

It was in this world of scholarship, both worldly and religious, that Daniel, Hananiah, Mishael, and Azariah were to move and function in the "king's service" (Dan. 1:19) after their three years of training.

Induction into the King's Service

Shalom M. Paul[14] calls attention to an eighteenth-century BC letter written in the Akkadian language, sent to Shibtu, the highest ranking wife of Zimri-lim, king of Mari. Mari was a city located on the Euphrates River some 250 miles north of the city of Babylon. Zimri-lim ruled Mari from 1775 to 1761 BC. Shibtu carried out administrative duties on the king's behalf for the city, palace, and temple during his absence (often when away at war). Even though this letter originated several hundred years earlier than the time of Daniel and his three friends in the sixth century BC, Shalom Paul observes that Daniel 1 "shares a remarkable stage by stage correlation with" this letter from Mari, "describing the procedure of induction into court service."[15] These correlations are shown in figure 6.1:

	Mari Letter	**Daniel 1**
Candidates	Female; selected from war captives brought to the capital city of Mari	Male; selected from war captives brought to the capital city of Babylon (v. 3)
Unique Skills	Weavers	"skillful in all wisdom, knowing knowledge, understanding/perceiving knowledge" (v. 4, AT)
Outstanding Physical Features	"beautiful women who, from the tip of their toe to the hair of their head, have no blemish"[16]	"young men without any physical defect, handsome" (v. 4)

---

14. Paul, "Mesopotamian Babylonian Background," in *Book of Daniel*, 1:62-63.
15. Ibid., 62.
16. Ibid.

Supervisors' Names Mentioned	Waradillishum; Mukannishum	Ashpenaz (v. 3); "the guard" (vv. 11, 16)[17]
Purpose of Selection	"to become adept at singing Subarean music"[18]	"to teach them the literature and language of the Kasdim" (v. 4, AT)
Status Officially Changed	From weavers to singers	"to enter the king's service" (v. 5)
Special Food Portions Mentioned	"pay heed to their food allotment"[19]	"daily amount of food and wine from the king's table" (v. 5)
Purpose of Special Food Portions	"so that their countenance does not change"[20]	Lest "their faces would look less healthy" (v. 10, AT)

Fig. 6.1. Correlation between Mari letter and Daniel 1

Ten Times (Dan. 1:20)

When King Nebuchadnezzar examined Daniel, Hananiah, Mishael, and Azariah at the conclusion of their three-year study of Babylonian literature and wisdom, he found them to be "ten times better than [lit. "above"] all the magicians[, that is,] the enchanters in all his realm" (v. 20, AT). The New International Version's "magicians and enchanters" (and other English versions) misses the subtlety of the Hebrew here. There is no conjunction "and" between the two nouns; the Hebrew has "the magicians the enchanters," implying *one* group called by two names: "the magicians, that is, the enchanters."

The expression "ten times" is not to be taken as an exact number, but as "many," "much," or "superior." Other instances of the use of "ten times" in this sense in the Old Testament are the following:

17. See the sidebar "'The Guard' and the Meaning of Cognate," in "The Story" section above, p. 51.
18. Paul, "Mesopotamian Babylonian Background," in *Book of Daniel*, 1:63.
19. Ibid.
20. Ibid.

1. Jacob said to his wives, "Your father has cheated me by changing my wages ten times." He later made this charge to Laban face to face: "You changed my wages ten times" (Gen. 31:7, 41).

2. During their escape from Egypt to Canaan, God declared that those "who disobeyed me and tested me ten times—not one of them will ever see the land I promised" (Num. 14:22-23).

3. In postexilic Judah, Nehemiah and his work crew were rebuilding the walls of Jerusalem. Some non-Jewish locals, headed by a couple of fellows named Sanballat and Tobiah, opposed this project. They were planning to kill the Jewish workers and put a stop to the rebuilding work. But the Jewish workers reported to Nehemiah that some Jewish sympathizers who lived among these rabble-rousers "came and warned [lit. "said to"] us ten times, 'Wherever you turn, they are against you'" (Neh. 4:12 [v. 6 HB], AT). So Nehemiah posted extra guards with "swords, spears and bows" to protect the workers (v. 13 [7 HB]).

4. In one of his speeches to suffering Job, Bildad obliquely hinted that Job is "a wicked man" (Job 18:5), "an evil man," and "one who does not know God" (v. 21). Job rather indignantly replied, "How long will you torment me and crush me with words? Ten times now you have reproached me; shamelessly you attack me" (19:2-3).

God behind the Scenes

Daniel 1:2

And the Lord ["the Sovereign One" or "Adonay"] gave into his [i.e., Nebuchadnezzar's] power [lit. "hand"] Jehoiakim king of Judah and some of the vessels of the temple [lit. "house"] of God. And he brought them [i.e., the vessels] to the temple [lit. "house"] of his gods in the land of Shinar [i.e., Babylon] and put them into the treasure house of his gods. (AT)

In this verse, most English versions say "his god" (singular) when referring to Nebuchadnezzar's deity. The Hebrew word is grammatically plural, which when referring to Israel's deity *is* considered singular (God) but when referring to deity of non-Israelites is usually considered plural (gods). In the somewhat brief historical document of Nebuchadnezzar's feats that is available to us, he speaks of "Marduk, my lord" twice and "Marduk, my king" once. But he also speaks of having enhanced "the city of Babylon" along with "the sanctuaries of my lords Nebo and Marduk" and of "(trusting) in the power of my lords Nebo and Marduk."[21] Nebuchadnezzar's allegiance, then, is to two deities into whose sanctuary treasuries he may have stored the Jerusalem temple vessels. Thus I have translated "his gods" (twice).

No credit, therefore, was to be given to the gods Nebo and Marduk for what seemed to the Judeans a disastrous loss and to Nebuchadnezzar a great victory. This event was the will of Adonay, whom the Judeans called Sovereign.

Daniel 1:9

"Now God [Elohim] extended/maintained [lit. "gave"] loyalty [*hesed*] and compassion to/with Daniel in the presence of the chief official" (AT). The grammatical structure of the Hebrew of this sentence does not indicate that God caused *the chief official* to favor Daniel (as the NIV and most English versions indicate) but rather that *God* maintained *his* loyalty (*hesed*) to Daniel. One may compare Joseph in the Egyptian prison: While there, "the LORD [Yahweh] was with Joseph, and he extended to him loyalty [*hesed*] and showed him favor/grace in the eyes of the prison warden" (Gen. 39:21, AT).

Daniel had just requested of the Babylonian chief official that he be allowed to refrain from partaking of the king's food and wine so that he might not defile himself (Dan. 1:8). In light of the fact that such a request is all but certain to be refused, John Goldingay comments: "Daniel's demonstration of his commitments is matched by God's own. In the story, it begins

---

21. *Ancient Near Eastern Texts*, 307.

to look as if things will turn out all right because of who God is, as well as of who Daniel is."[22] Goldingay's "because of who God is" is reflected in the word "loyalty" in my translation of Daniel 1:9 above. "Loyalty" expresses the primary meaning of the Hebrew word *ḥesed*.[23] The essence of God's character is that he is loyal to humans who are loyal to him.

Thus, even though Ashpenaz fears for his life—"'my head' is at stake," he says (v. 10, AT)—it is Daniel's God who, because he is on the side of Daniel and the other three Judean young men (see v. 11), is orchestrating the whole "test" that Daniel suggested (v. 12). Because God is loyal to a loyal Daniel, God is committed to subverting the command of the king who believes *he* is in charge of everything.

Daniel 1:17

"To these four young men God [Elohim] gave knowledge and insight in all literature and wisdom" (AT). The four Judean young men may certainly have had natural intellectual abilities for learning new languages and grasping the flow of historical events and even the meanings of astrological formations. But to discern the divine significance in all this, only the God who created all and directs the flow of history could reveal its eternal significance.

The Story's Relationship, If Any, to the Other Five Stories or Four Visions in Daniel

Faithfulness

Jim Edlin points out that story one in Daniel 1 is related to Daniel 3 and 6, since all three chapters present a "test of faithfulness." He further suggests that in all three of these chapters the three young Israelite men are tested "to maintain religious conviction in the midst of a hostile environment." "Severe consequences" are threatened if they will not compromise, if they insist on

---

22. Goldingay, *Daniel*, 169.

23. *Dictionary of Classical Hebrew*, ed. David J. A. Clines (Sheffield, UK: Sheffield Phoenix, 1993), 3:277, Oaktree Software/Accordance; *New International Dictionary of Old Testament Theology and Exegesis*, ed. Willem A. VanGemeren (Grand Rapids: Zondervan, 1997), 2:206, Oaktree Software/Accordance.

"holding on to their beliefs." These consequences entail being rejected at the royal precincts (ch. 1), being burned to a crisp in a fiery furnace (ch. 3), and becoming lions' food (ch. 6). Yet, in the face of these dire consequences, "they choose the more difficult route and remain faithful to their convictions": no eating of royal table meat, no worshipping an idol, and continuing their worship of God. To these four young men who showed this depth of faithfulness, God in turn showed his absolute faithfulness to them.[24]

"Vessels from the Temple of God"

As noted in verse 2, Nebuchadnezzar confiscated some vessels from God's temple in Jerusalem and took them with him when he returned to Babylon. There, he put them "in the treasure house of his gods" (AT). (See my discussion of "god" and "gods," in subsection titled "Daniel 1:2," in section titled "God behind the Scenes," pp. 58-59.)

The mention and placement of these confiscated vessels in the Babylonian temple's treasury "anticipates the story of Daniel 5."[25] There we find Babylonian "King Belshazzar" in the midst of a "great banquet for a thousand of his nobles," to which he had also brought "his wives and his concubines" (5:1-2). It seems that Belshazzar was already somewhat drunk, for the author says, "While Belshazzar was drinking his wine," he demanded that someone bring "the gold and silver goblets that Nebuchadnezzar his father had taken from the temple in Jerusalem" (v. 2). The purpose was so they might all drink wine from them and, while doing so, praise the "gods of gold and silver, of bronze, iron, wood and stone" (v. 4).

---

24. Edlin, *Daniel*, 45.
25. Tremper Longman III, *Daniel*, The NIV Application Commentary (Grand Rapids: Zondervan, 1999), 46, Kindle.

Faithful Living Today

Adverse Circumstances

At first read, it appears that Daniel and his three colleagues have met with disastrous circumstances: kidnapped from their homes and taken from all that has up to then given meaning to their lives—families, language, food, place of worship, friends, and more—then transported hundreds of miles away. In that new place, they find a language spoken they did not readily understand, customs they were not used to, and all their decisions and moves subject to the orders of others. Yet the author gives no hint that Daniel or his three colleagues grumbled or showed any resentment against their captors. They did not whine, "Why, God?" nor did they live in a constant state of "if only," longing for the way things used to be "back home."

It seems that Daniel and his colleagues quickly accepted that their new circumstance of Babylonian captivity had not happened by accident. It was *their* God, whose wisdom is greater than theirs, who had put them there. Though they did not see early on God's larger plan for the Babylonian Empire (and those to follow), they were willing to fit into his plan and be used in any way he chose.

Though most of us who read this book most likely will not be carried off into foreign captivity (though perhaps some will), adverse circumstances will and do sometimes engulf us. Will our faith then be strong in the one who is right there with us in the adverse circumstance and, though we may not see it at the time, intends good? (See Gen. 50:20.)

7

Story Two (Dan. 2)

Summary

Babylonian king Nebuchadnezzar had dreams that troubled his spirit, preventing sleep. When called to do so, his astrologers and other such experts in his employ were unable to reveal to him either the dream itself or its meaning. Threatened with death as punishment, just in the nick of time the God of heaven revealed to Daniel both the dream itself and its meaning.

The Story

The author places story two "in the second year of" Nebuchadnezzar's reign as king of Babylon and its large and expanding empire (Dan. 2:1). The king was not presently away with his army waging war against some distant rebellious kingdom (of which, in fact, there were many). Rather, he was at home in his royal palace, sleeping in his royal bedroom, in his royal bed. But the king couldn't sleep. Why? Because he has been dreaming dreams, such that "his spirit was agitated" (v. 1, AT).

The author speaks of "dreams" in the plural (v. 1), perhaps hinting that this may not be a single-night occurrence. It may be that Nebuchadnezzar has been dreaming the same dream for several nights. Dreams carried much significance in the ancient biblical world and often were considered as "means of divine revelation,"[1] whether from God or the gods. In Babylonia, however, this so-called divine revelation was to be found in a library collection of dream books. Specialists would search these dream books for parallels or precedents and then give an interpretation of a dream, usually dreams of persons in high positions, such as kings (see the subsection titled "Dreams and Dream Books in Mesopotamia and Egypt," in section titled "Customs and Practices Explained," p. 73).

So King Nebuchadnezzar called for the specialists, "the divination experts,"[2] to help him understand the meaning of his dreams and their significance for his kingdom. Most likely no one of the groups—the "magicians, enchanters, sorcerers and astrologers" (v. 2)—that the author lists here is especially engaged in dream interpretation. The group titles are generally synonymous for soothsayers important to the politics and religion of Babylon.[3] Of these groups, the one last mentioned, the "astrologers," the *Kasdim* (see subsection titled "The Kasdim [Dan. 1:4]," in section titled "Customs and Practices Explained," in ch. 6, "Story One [Dan. 1]," p. 55) seems to be the group that speaks for them all (see 2:4-5, 10).

Upon learning why the king has called them, the astrologers respectfully asked that he tell them the contents of his dream; they will then give its interpretation (v. 4). Imagine their shock when the king demanded that *they* tell *him* his dream, *then* give its interpretation! If they can't do this, he threatened, they will be "torn limb from limb" and their "houses will be turned into a rubbish heap" (v. 5, NASB). Still in shock, they asked a second time that their king tell them the content of his dream before they can interpret it (v. 7). The king in turn accused them of stalling, "trying to gain time" (v. 8). In complete bewilderment, the astrologers dared to remind the king that what he was asking no other king anywhere had ever asked of his

1. Goldingay, *Daniel*, 206.

2. A. Leo Oppenheim, *Ancient Mesopotamia: Portrait of a Dead Civilization*, rev. ed. (Chicago: University of Chicago Press, 1977), 81, Google Books.

3. Goldingay, *Daniel*, 197.

diviners. What they were saying is that the dream books do not reveal a person's *dreams*, but only the possible *meanings* of dreams.

The astrologers then revealed a truth that they themselves did not truly grasp: that only deity can reveal what the king has demanded. To these astrologers, deity was "the gods," and since these gods did not dwell among humankind, they were, in fact, inaccessible and silent (v. 11; see the sidebar "'The Gods' of King Nebuchadnezzar's Diviners" below).

"The Gods" of King Nebuchadnezzar's Diviners

By "the gods," these diviners were referring to the deities whose idols inhabited the temples and shrines in the cities throughout Mesopotamia. Indeed, the deities themselves did not dwell among humankind, as the diviners said (Dan. 2:11), but were believed to dwell in the heavens. But it was also believed that the gods in some way also indwelt their idols. The prophet of Isaiah 41:22-24 records Yahweh's challenge to the idols: "Tell us, you idols, what is going to happen. . . . Tell us what the future holds, so we may know that you are gods. . . . But you are less than nothing and your works are utterly worthless." In Isaiah 46:1, the prophet mocks two of the chief Babylonian gods, Bel and Nebo. With a bit of imagination, we see the two gods peering over the verandas of their heavenly palaces. They see on earth "their idols . . . borne by beasts of burden" (v. 1). John Oswalt observes "that these beautiful images . . . are now a matter for oxcarts and donkeys. What a decline—how the mighty gods are humiliated and ashamed."[4]

Yet, as the story unfolds, Daniel will reveal that there is indeed a God in heaven who operates among humankind and will reveal to Daniel exactly what the king is demanding.

Why did King Nebuchadnezzar make such an impossible demand of his counselors? On the one hand, perhaps he remembers the dream only vaguely, or none of the details at all, and is hoping that if they can tell him, the

---

4. John N. Oswalt, *The Book of Isaiah: Chapters 40–66*, The New International Commentary on the Old Testament (Grand Rapids: Eerdmans, 1998), 228.

dream images will again come into his mind. Because he had seen the dream repeatedly, he may think it must have some significance, not only for him as king but, *because* he is king, for his kingdom as well.

On the other hand, Nebuchadnezzar may well recall the details and images of his dreams and this is all an act, but an act that can well result in deadly consequences for his counselors. Goldingay suggests that the king is trying to determine if the counselors have discernment capabilities surpassing those of others.[5] Thus the king may think, "Fellows, if you tell me my dream, then what you say it means will hold water, and I'll sit up and take notice. Otherwise, I may as well call in some street sweepers and garbage collectors. Their opinions would be just as valid!"

The king's counselors' inability to meet his demand provoked the king to such anger and fury that he immediately ordered that all these counselors (Dan. 2:12 [NIV: "wise men of Babylon"]) be executed. Since "Daniel and his [three] friends," all recent graduates from their three years of Babylonian studies, were included in this elite group, they, too, were marked to be put to death (v. 13).

The executioner was "Arioch, the commander of the king's guard" (v. 14). As he was preparing to carry out the king's order, Daniel, who was not privy to the confrontation between the king and his counselors, asked Arioch for an explanation (v. 15). Upon being told the reason for the death order, Daniel "went in and requested from the king that he might grant him a set time to declare to the king the interpretation" (v. 16, AT).

Apparently Nebuchadnezzar granted Daniel's request, because Daniel returned to his house and told his friends the details of the king's execution order that threatened him and his friends along "with the rest of the wise men of Babylon" (v. 18). In response to this dire threat, Daniel and his friends did what will characterize their responses in the stories following: they did not try to flee or hide; rather, they turned to the "God of heaven

---

5. Goldingay, *Daniel*, 208.

concerning this mystery" (v. 18). The "mystery" refers to the details of the dream that Nebuchadnezzar either could not recall or was purposely hiding from his counselors.

Daniel urged his friends to request "mercy from the God of heaven" for both themselves and the other "wise men of Babylon," that the execution order might be stayed (v. 18). After all, these Babylonian wise men were innocent of any wrongdoing. They had acted within the bounds of their own years of training and human knowledge. They simply were not able, within human ability, to meet the king's demand.

Having interceded with the "God of heaven" concerning the "mystery," this God in whom they trusted responded quickly: "Then to Daniel in a vision of the night the vision was revealed. Then Daniel worshipped [lit. "knelt to"] the God of heaven" (v. 19, AT). He chanted or sang to God:

May the name of God be worshipped from eternity to eternity, the One to whom belongs wisdom and power. . . .

O God of my fathers, I am thanking and praising you, you who have given me wisdom and power.

You have now made known to me that which we asked from you, namely, the matter of the king you have made known to us. (Vv. 20, 23, AT)

Armed with this revelation from the God of heaven, Daniel hurried to Arioch and requested an audience with the king. Arioch informed the king that he has found "a man from the exiles of Judah" (v. 25, AT), who made known to him the meaning of his dream.

But it's not only the meaning of the dream that the king wants to know but also the dream itself. Is this Daniel any different from all the other counselors? So the king's line of questioning to Daniel is the same as to his other counselors: "Do you possess the ability to tell me the dream which I saw and its interpretation?" (v. 26, AT). Daniel's reply was a frank "No. I'm no more able than any wise man, enchanter, magician, or diviner in your kingdom to explain your mystery" (v. 27, AT).

Can't you just hear the king's heart do a flip on that one? "Why on earth did Arioch bring me *this* flunky?" Then Daniel said a startling thing, something the king had not heard before: "But! There is a God in heaven, a revealer of mysteries." Daniel continued, "He has made known to King Nebuchadnezzar that which is to happen in the coming days" (v. 28, AT).

Daniel then proceeded to tell King Nebuchadnezzar what the "revealer of mysteries" had first "showed" the king in his dream and then "revealed" to him (Daniel) (vv. 29-30). This was not, said Daniel, because he, himself, possessed "greater wisdom" than others, but so that he might help the king understand what (implied) God was saying to him (v. 30).

Essentially, what King Nebuchadnezzar saw in his dream was "an enormous, dazzling statue" (v. 31). It had a head of pure gold, a chest and arms of silver, a belly and thighs of bronze, and legs of iron. Its feet were weird: a mixture of iron and baked clay (vv. 32-33).

What the king saw next was even stranger. A rock that had been quarried "without hands" (AT [the Aramaic text does not have "human"]) came from somewhere; the Aramaic text of verse 45 clarifies that the rock "was quarried from the mountain" (AT), though it does not say *what* mountain. The rock struck this enormous statue on its feet—its weakest point (v. 34). So, poof! The entire statue shattered into nothing but tiny powder-like bits that Daniel likened to "chaff on a threshing floor" that the wind whisks away (v. 35). The rock itself, however, was like a living thing: it grew in size until it "became a huge mountain and filled the whole earth" (v. 35).

"Without hands" does seem to imply that no *human* rock cutter had been involved in quarrying this rock, so the New International Version's supplying of "human" is interpretively correct. This also, then, would seem to imply that the divine was involved. In fact, verses 44-45 clarify that it was the "God of heaven" who was the power behind this whole rock affair.

So the details of the dream itself have been told. The takeaway from this, as John Goldingay observes, must be viewed against the "despairing assumption of the [Babylonian] experts"[6] of verse 11, who said, "No one can reveal [such things] . . . except the gods." Their point was that since "they [the gods] do not live among humans," their knowledge is unavailable to humans. But the irony in Daniel's report to the king is that there is, in fact, a God—Daniel's God—who *does* reveal secrets.[7]

Between the conclusion of Daniel's relating the details of the king's dream (v. 35) and his launching into the interpretation of that dream (v. 36), the author gives no indication of Nebuchadnezzar's reaction. Is he awed? Surprised? Disbelieving? Does Daniel's description match up with what he himself may remember of his own dream? Jim Edlin suggests,

> The lack of response from the king at this point is a subtle indicator that the balance of power has shifted from Nebuchadnezzar to the man of God. The king who dominated the conversation in the opening scene (vv 1-13) remains quiet while Daniel speaks. This element supports the theme of the dream that earthly powers give way to the divine kingdom.[8]

Daniel then turned to the interpretation of King Nebuchadnezzar's dream. He ascribed to Nebuchadnezzar the title "king of kings" and said that he was the "head of gold" of the dream's statue (vv. 37-38). As such, affirmed Daniel, Nebuchadnezzar was privileged to exercise authority over "humankind wherever they dwell" and even over the "animals of the field and the birds of the sky" (v. 38, AT). This was a derived authority, given him by the "God of heaven" (v. 37). Nebuchadnezzar was to be "ruler over them all" (v. 38). We hear an allusion "to the creation story of Gen 1,"[9] in which God gave this authority to the whole of "mankind ['ādām]" (v. 26). Jim Edlin further suggests that "Daniel confirms what Jeremiah believed. Nebuchadnezzar is God's servant who does only what God allows him to do (Jer 25:9)."[10] Indeed, Nebuchadnezzar himself saw his authority extending

6. Goldingay, *Daniel*, 213.
7. Ibid.
8. Edlin, *Daniel*, 80.
9. Ibid.
10. Ibid.

worldwide. In one of his inscriptions we read, "O merciful Marduk, may the house I have built endure forever, may I . . . receive therein tribute of the kings of all regions, from all mankind."[11]

Daniel's expression "humankind wherever they dwell" (v. 38, AT) and Nebuchadnezzar's inscription "from all mankind," however, must be viewed within the geographical extent of the lands Nebuchadnezzar ruled during his years on the Babylonian throne. His geographical empire was small in comparison to that of later Persian Cyrus, whose borders reached eastward to the border of India and westward to Greece and Egypt.

Daniel then spoke of a (second) kingdom that would arise following Nebuchadnezzar's kingdom, though it would be "inferior" (v. 39). It was represented by the silver chest and arms of the dream's statue (see v. 32). This kingdom then would be followed by a third kingdom of bronze that "will rule over the whole earth" (v. 39), represented by the thighs of the dream's statue (see v. 32). This kingdom in turn would be followed by a fourth kingdom "strong as iron" (v. 40), represented by the legs, feet, and toes of the dream's statue (see v. 33). Though iron is the strongest of the four metals, however, this fourth kingdom is inherently weakened by the clay that is mixed with the iron; though it is extremely powerful, it surprisingly is easily broken.[12]

Daniel then explained the meaning of the "rock cut out of a mountain, but not by human hands" (v. 45). This rock is God's kingdom, a kingdom that the "God of heaven will set up" (v. 44). It will be indestructible and will "endure forever" (v. 44). Its inception is "in the time of those kings" but crushing the kingdoms represented by the various parts and metals of the giant statue (v. 44). Jim Edlin comments:

> This explains why Daniel's [earlier] description of the dream mentioned that all the kingdoms were destroyed "at the same time" (v 35). Daniel is not suggesting that God's kingdom enters this world at one specific time

11. Michael Kerrigan, *Ancient Peoples in Their Own Words: Ancient Writing from Tomb Hieroglyphs to Roman Graffiti* (New York: Sterling, 2019), 39.

12. Goldingay, *Daniel*, 203.

but that it continues to emerge within the framework of human realms.
. . . The kingdom of God flourishes in spite of apparent realities.

. . . The kingdom of God supersedes human kingdoms. It endures
whereas earthly kingdoms do not.[13]

Daniel wrapped up the revelation of Nebuchadnezzar's dream and its
interpretation with a denial of any innate personal power. He declared, "A
great God has made known to the king what shall be after this" (v. 45, ESV).
"A great God" is *'ĕlāh rab/v* in Aramaic (*'ĕlāh* [God]; *rab/v* [great]) and may
have been in Daniel's mind a *title* for God, pronounced *EHlah Rahv*. Thus
Daniel has declared to Nebuchadnezzar that it was not one of the gods of
Babylon who was communicating with him (Daniel) throughout the previous sleepless night. Rather, it was *Ehlah Rav* (Great God). Therefore, the
king can now rest assured that "the dream is certain, and its interpretation
sure" (v. 45, ESV).

King Nebuchadnezzar was so emotionally overcome at this revelation of
the "mystery" of his dream that he "fell upon his face [lit. "upon his nose"]
and paid homage to Daniel" (v. 46, ESV). Then, as if Daniel were himself
deity, he "said that an offering of incense should be poured out to him" (v.
46, AT). Yet Nebuchadnezzar, this great king of the Babylonian Empire,
did acknowledge that Daniel was merely the human conduit for his (Daniel's) God, whom he acknowledged to be "the God of gods and the Lord of
kings" (v. 47). Daniel's God, he marveled, was "a revealer of mysteries" (v.
47). Indeed, Deity had spoken into the realm of humankind! (v. 47; see v. 11).

The addendum to this story is that King Nebuchadnezzar tangibly
awarded Daniel with a position of high political authority as "ruler over the
entire province of Babylon" and even gave him authority over all the various
groups of the king's counselors (v. 48). From this position, Daniel requested
administrative appointments for his three friends, Shadrach, Meshach, and
Abednego, which the king granted (v. 49). Daniel would certainly not have

---

13. Edlin, *Daniel*, 81.

left them unrewarded, for, after all, they had earlier supported him in a night of prayer, pleading with the "God of heaven" for the "mystery" of the king's dream to be revealed to Daniel (see vv. 17-19). These appointments were not without danger, however. Possibly because they were not native Babylonians but rather merely "exiles from Judah" (v. 25), and certainly because of their loyalty to Israel's one God, these four Judeans will become targets of intense jealousy, with schemes calling for their deaths (see Dan. 3 and 6).

Customs and Practices Explained

The Babylonian Three-Year Training and the Babylonian System of Royal Dating (Dan. 2:1)

The three-year training period for Daniel and his three colleagues appears to have begun soon after their arrival in Babylon, which most likely would have been during King Nebuchadnezzar's first year of reign. Yet the story of Daniel interpreting the king's dream in Daniel 2 is said to have occurred in the king's second year of reign (v. 1). One assumes that Daniel 2 follows Daniel 1 *chronologically*—that is, the dream interpretation story happens subsequent to Daniel's graduation from his three years of training. The question scholars have asked is, How can three years be squeezed into two? Any suggestion or scheme has its difficulties, but over a century ago S. R. Driver proposed that the author may be using the Assyrian-Babylonian way of reckoning a king's regnal years. In this system, the year in which the king ascended to the throne (his accession year) is not counted. Rather, the counting begins with "the first full year afterwards"[14]—that is, his first year begins with the first New Year celebration following his ascension to the throne.

---

14. S. R. Driver, *The Book of Daniel* (Cambridge, UK: Cambridge University, 1900), 17, Internet Archive, https://archive.org/details/bookdaniel00unkngoog/page/n131/mode/2up.

Based upon this Assyrian-Babylonian system, Jim Edlin explains how Daniel's three-year training can be reckoned within the first two years of Nebuchadnezzar's reign,[15] as shown in figure 7.1.

Daniel's First Training Year	= Nebuchadnezzar's Accession Year (Elul 605–Nisan 604 BC)
Daniel's Second Training Year	= Nebuchadnezzar's First Regnal Year (Nisan 604–Nisan 603 BC)
Daniel's Third Training Year	= Nebuchadnezzar's Second Regnal Year (Nisan 603–Nisan 602 BC)

Fig. 7.1. Daniel's training coordinated with Nebuchadnezzar's reign

Dreams and Dream Books in Mesopotamia and Egypt

Dreams were considered as events not to be treated lightly in ancient Mesopotamia and other ancient cultures. It was believed that dreams often carried messages from the gods, but such messages must be interpreted by specialists trained in the art of dream interpretation. Such interpretation "was treated as a science by philosophers and physicians."[16]

Ancient Mesopotamia and Egypt yield significant sources for written evidence of dream interpretation. These sources are "inscriptions, literary documents, letters, funerary texts, and dream-books."[17] When we say "dream books," they were not *books* in the sense of modern books, but rather clay tablets inscribed with writing. These dream tablets also contain an accumulation of images that have appeared in the previous dreams of people, along with the meanings and interpretations that the earlier dream interpreters have ascribed to them. So at any given time a specialist or specialists in dream interpretation could consult these dream tablets for precedents, somewhat like modern-day lawyers or judges consult precedents in law decisions and applications. Precedent dream images and their interpretations would help a specialist render an interpretation of the current dream.

---

15. Edlin, *Daniel*, 66.
16. J. Donald Hughes, "Dream Interpretation in Ancient Civilizations," in *Dreaming* 10, no. 1 (2000): 18.
17. Ibid., 7.

Examples of dream books are as follows: (1) From Mesopotamia, a notable dream book, containing a variety of topics, is from the library of the Assyrian king Ashurbanipal (r. 668-627 BC). (2) From Egypt is a dream book originating in the Twelfth Dynasty (2000–1800 BC), but the copy we have dates from the Nineteenth Dynasty (ca. 1300 BC).[18]

Ancient Middle Eastern Use of Wild and Domestic Animals

John Goldingay suggests that underlying Daniel's reference to King Nebuchadnezzar's rulership over the animals and birds may be the "eastern monarchs' establishing of game parks for captured wild animals."[19] A. Leo Oppenheim lists a number of domesticated fowls and other animals that are cited in various Mesopotamian royal texts: geese, ducks, a type of partridge, and others. The fowler or bird keeper is frequently mentioned. Fattening of birds with dough was practiced. Dogs were domesticated as pets and as helpers of shepherds. Lions were both kept in cages and hunted. Royal hunters also hunted elephants, wild bulls, and ostriches. At times these wild animals were kept in parks and were a point of royal pride. Monkeys from India and Africa are mentioned. In one of the Amarna letters a Babylonian king requested of the Egyptian pharaoh Amenophis IV lifelike specimens of Egyptian "animals that live either on land or in the river," most likely meaning the crocodile or hippopotamus. These would possibly have been stuffed.[20]

God behind the Scenes

Daniel 2:18-19, 28, 36, and 44

In four of these verses Daniel identified Israel's God by the title the "God of heaven." The exception is verse 28, when Daniel affirmed to King Nebuchadnezzar, "There is *a God in heaven* who reveals mysteries" (emphasis added). The story of chapter 2 unfolds on Daniel's belief that behind the

---

18. Ibid., 7-10.
19. Goldingay, *Daniel*, 202.
20. Oppenheim, *Ancient Mesopotamia*, 46-48.

outworking of the events of human history, there is, in fact, a God who "is both transcendent and immanent."[21] By this is meant that although the title in verse 28 agrees somewhat with what the astrologers affirmed in verse 11 about the gods not residing with humans, there is also an acknowledgment of God's accessibility, since he, the God in heaven, reveals mysteries to humans on earth.[22]

The Story's Relationship, If Any, to the Other Five Stories or Four Visions in Daniel

Most scholars interpret the different parts or metals of Nebuchadnezzar's dream statue as representing four kingdoms. There is significant disagreement among them, however, concerning the identification of these kingdoms. There is insufficient space in this book to present the various schemes scholars have offered.

A number of scholars have suggested that Daniel 7 interprets the four kingdoms of Daniel 2. Thus the two chapters are seen as parallel. Jim Edlin suggests, however, that though the two chapters are parallel in many ways, "their content is not necessarily synonymous."[23] He further suggests,

Four is used in biblical literature to suggest completeness. . . . It may well be that the four kingdoms of this dream indicate the totality of human kingdoms, whatever that number may actually turn out to be. The fourth kingdom would be the final kingdom of humankind. . . . The final kingdom of this world, like the rest, will come to an end. Throughout the rise and fall of kingdoms the rule of God will continue.

Faithful Living Today

We in America (where this book was written and published) in the early twenty-first century AD do not live under the oppressive dictates of

---

21. Edlin, *Daniel*, 75.
22. Goldingay, *Daniel*, 199.
23. Edlin, *Daniel*, 82.

totalitarianism. Yet there are violent satanic forces loose in our land whose goals are to destroy Christian values of marriage, family, church, and public life. We will be encouraged to read Tremper Longman's comment of what the essential message of Daniel 2 is: "Though circumstances appear to favor the power of ungodly personalities and institutions, God will overpower them."[24]

24. Longman, *Daniel*, 88.

8

Story Three (Dan. 3)

Summary

Story three (Dan. 3) features Daniel's three Judean colleagues, Shadrach, Meshach, and Abednego, mentioned by name thirteen times. Opposing them is Babylon's supreme ruler, mentioned nineteen times as "King Nebuchadnezzar," "Nebuchadnezzar," "the king," and "O King" (most versions, but NIV: "Your Majesty"). The plot unfolds around "an image of gold, sixty cubits [ninety feet] high and six cubits [nine feet] wide" (v. 1) that the king had erected and then ordered that all "provincial officials" should attend its dedication (v. 3). This would include Daniel's three Judean colleagues, who earlier had been awarded positions as "administrators over the province of Babylon" (2:49). At the dedication, all persons would be required to fall prostrate in worship before this gold image. Disobedience would be punished with immediate death in a "blazing furnace" (3:6). The story, then, unfolds around this question: Will these three Judean provincial officials remain faithful to their commitment to serve and worship only the "Most High God" (v. 26) or, in the interest of saving their lives, capitulate and worship the king's image of gold?

The Story

The author does not give us any hint of when during Nebuchadnezzar's reign this story took place. We are told that "King Nebuchadnezzar made an image of gold, sixty cubits [ninety feet] high and six cubits [nine feet] wide, and set it up on the plain of Dura in the province of Babylon" (Dan. 3:1). No researcher knows the location of Dura, but that is of little importance to the overall significance of the story.

There are two connections between this story of Daniel 3 and Nebuchadnezzar's dream story of Daniel 2 that should be noted at the outset.

The *first connection* is that the author of Daniel uses the same Aramaic word, *ṣĕlēm*, for both "statue" in 2:31 (and elsewhere) and "image" in 3:1 (and elsewhere). It is the translators of the New International Version who choose to translate the Aramaic word differently in the two chapters, and thus the point is missed that the author is hinting at something significant: "statue" and "image" are to be associated.

The *second connection* is that the head of Nebuchadnezzar's dream statue of Daniel 2 was made of gold (v. 32), and figuratively, Nebuchadnezzar was "that head of gold" (v. 38). Nebuchadnezzar's image of Daniel 3 was also made of gold (v. 1). If this image represents Nebuchadnezzar himself, as some scholars suggest, then the "gold" points to his own fragility—he and his kingdom will not last forever. If it represents one of the Babylonian gods, as others suggest (Nebuchadnezzar's favorite god was Bel), then it points to this god's powerlessness—it or he will be bested by a Deity (God) who is supremely superior. John Goldingay observes that it makes no difference if the statue symbolizes the king or the king's god; the king erected it as a display of the king's authority and to oppose the weakness suggested by the Daniel 2 imagery.[1]

The author of story three was perhaps saying more than at first meets one's eye when he said in verse 1, "King Nebuchadnezzar made [*ăbad*] an image of gold." The Aramaic verb *ăbad* also means "to serve," such as a slave who serves a master or a person who performs acts of worship before a god or God. Thus, suggests Jim Edlin, this story's opening line could also be read,

---

1. Goldingay, *Daniel*, 236.

"King Nebuchadnezzar served an image of gold." Edlin then adds, "The one who thinks he commands power through his creation may in fact be subservient to that very creation." He then draws attention to "Isaiah's satire of the deluded idol maker."[2] In that satire, the prophet speaks of a person who cuts down a tree of the forest: "With some of it he kindles a fire and warms himself, bakes bread . . . roasts his meat and eats his fill. . . . The rest of it he fashions into a god, for his idol; he bows down to it and worships, praying to it, saying, 'Save me, because my god are you!'" (Isa. 44:15-17, AT).

So, like Isaiah's self-deluded idol maker, in the self-assurance of his own absolute sovereignty, Nebuchadnezzar decided to throw a huge festival to celebrate the dedication of his golden image, to which all officials of Nebuchadnezzar's empire were to attend; the text literally says "He sent to gather," so the New International Version's "summoned" well expresses the spirit of the invitation (Dan. 3:2). The invitation included all, from the "satraps" at the highest level to the "magistrates" at the lowest, and any others under the catchall phrase "provincial officials" (vv. 2-3).

A great fanfare of musical instruments was to accompany the dedication ceremony. An orchestra consisting of three kinds of wind instruments (horns, flutes, and pipes) and three kinds of stringed instruments (zithers, lyres, and harps) are mentioned, plus "all kinds of music," whatever that may entail. What a cacophony of sound that was to be (v. 5a)!

But this cacophony of music was not to be for the mere esthetic enjoyment of the many ceremony attendees. Rather, this royal orchestra was to function as a collective worship leader, for this was not merely a political rally. In reality it was a *worship* rally, for upon hearing the cacophonous sound of this royal orchestra, all attendees, so the herald announced (v. 4; lit. "read [or "called out"] with strength [i.e., "loudly"]"), "must fall down and worship the image of gold" (v. 5b). The penalty for anyone failing or refusing to do so would be immediate death in "a blazing furnace" (v. 6).

---

2. Edlin, *Daniel*, 92.

So, who would *not* obey the command of the herald? All King Nebu-chadnezzar's subjects from "all the nations and peoples of every language," knowing that this command came from King Nebuchadnezzar, in obedience to his sovereignty, "fell down and worshiped the image" (v. 7). Or did they? Were there no holdouts?

Well, yes, there were—three, in fact—those same three Judean exiles, Shadrach, Meshach, and Abednego, who, in story one (Dan. 1), had declined the food and wine from the king's table. They were now also resisting the king's edict to worship the gold image! Their resistance did not go unno-ticed. "Some astrologers" had been watching them and snitched on them to King Nebuchadnezzar: "They neither serve your gods nor worship the image of gold you have set up" (3:8, 12).

These "astrologers" were among the king's advisory groups mentioned earlier (see 2:2 et al.) and were professional colleagues of these three Judeans. What was their motive for spying on them and snitching to the king? We can probably chalk it up to professional jealousy.[3] After all, how did these three Judean foreigners warrant administrative positions "over the province of Babylon" (see 2:49)?

The astrologers' snitching to the king produced the response they want-ed. Nebuchadnezzar was "furious with rage" that anyone would dare to defy his edict (3:13). Ordering Shadrach, Meshach, and Abednego to come before him, he demanded they worship his image or suffer the consequence of being tossed into the blazing furnace. Then, sneeringly, he challenged them, "Then who is [the] god who could rescue you from my hand?" (v. 15, AT). This challenge echoes Assyrian king Sennacherib's challenge to Judah's king Hezekiah a century earlier: "Who among all the gods of these lands have saved their land from my hand, that the LORD [*yhwh*] would save Jerusalem from my hand?" (Isa. 36:20, NASB; see also 2 Kings 18:35). In fact, it is *only* "the LORD [*yhwh*]," whom long ago, just before God's people had crossed the

---

3. Goldingay, *Daniel*, 233.

Jordan into Canaan, Moses had declared to be "the Rock," "faithful God," "Father," "Creator," and "Most High," who could declare, "There is no god besides me . . . and no one can deliver out of my hand" (Deut. 32:4, 6, 8, 39). This is the God whom these three Judean holdouts worshipped.

Shadrach, Meshach, and Abednego did not back down before the king's fury. They simply stated their position: "If it happens, our God, whom we serve, is able to rescue us from the blazing furnace, and from your hand, O King, he will rescue [us]. But if not, may it be known to you, O King, that your gods we will not serve, and the image of gold that you have erected we will not worship" (Dan. 3:17-18, AT).

These three Judeans' intransient stance of noncompliance infuriated Nebuchadnezzar even more, such that the "image of his face" (AT [NIV: "his attitude"]) toward them changed (v. 19). Perhaps the author intends a bit of irony here in that the Aramaic word for "image" is *ṣĕlēm*, the same as previously used for Nebuchadnezzar's "image of gold" (v. 1 et al.). One can visualize the king's twisted face and bulging eyes as he is unable to comprehend such defiance by three underlings at his royal self, the most powerful person in the entire world! So commensurate with the rise of the heat of his fury, "he ordered the furnace heated seven times hotter than usual" (v. 19), "which was a way of saying that it was brought to its maximum temperature."[4]

Thus, with no further ado, the king ordered some of his "strongest soldiers" to bind ropes around Shadrach, Meshach, and Abednego, clothes and all, and toss them into the furnace (v. 20). This they do with alacrity, but the executioners' "loyalty to a godless and foolish king brings death,"[5] for the furnace's flames were so hot that they "killed the soldiers" as the three Judean men were falling into the midst of the furnace (v. 22).

Suddenly, all changed! King Nebuchadnezzar, watching the execution, suddenly leaped up, exclaiming that surely they had tied up and thrown only *three* men into the furnace, and yet now he was watching "four men walking

---

4. Edlin, *Daniel*, 98.
5. Longman, *Daniel*, 102.

around in the fire, unbound and unharmed" (v. 25). Goldingay suggests that apparently only Nebuchadnezzar saw this fourth figure. Who this fourth figure was is not clear. From the king's exclamation, it seems that he understood this figure in some sense to be divine (vv. 24-25) (see the sidebar "'Like a Son of the Gods' [Dan. 3:25]," p. 83). In verse 28, Nebuchadnezzar identified him as God's "angel." Goldingay draws attention to Psalm 34:7 (v. 8 HB), in which the psalmist affirms that "the angel of the LORD [*yhwh*] encamps around those who fear him, and he delivers them," and observes that the three Judeans and their deliverer in the furnace appear to be freely taking an enjoyable stroll in a garden.[6]

The three Judean men apparently had been tossed into the furnace through an opening at its top. Nebuchadnezzar, however, appears to be observing the four persons inside the furnace through a door or opening in its side at ground level. Nebuchadnezzar approached this door, rather carefully one would suppose because of the great heat, and called out, "Shadrach, Meshach and Abednego, servants of the Most High God, come out! Come here!" (Dan. 3:26). The king was not there alone, for the execution of these three Judeans who dared to defy the most powerful ruler in the world was being watched by all those officers and leaders who had gathered from all over the empire for the golden statue's dedication. Though the "astrologers" who had plotted the death of these three Judean exiles are not mentioned in the list of dignitaries in verse 27, they surely would have been there and would have witnessed their plot's failure. Responding to the king's call, Shadrach, Meshach, and Abednego came walking out of the furnace, unbound, unharmed in body, their hair unsinged, their clothes unscorched, and not even smelling of fire! (vv. 26-27).

The golden image is no longer the focus of the story. It is now a nobody, a nothing. Instead, Nebuchadnezzar gave praise to the Judean exiles' God, rather than to his golden image. Their commitment to serve their God

---

6. Goldingay, *Daniel*, 240.

regardless of the outcome led to Nebuchadnezzar granting Judaism recognition as a religion to be tolerated and respected.[7] Throughout his kingdom, this most powerful ruler in the world decreed that any "who say anything against the God of Shadrach, Meshach and Abednego [shall] be cut into pieces and their houses [shall] be turned into piles of rubble" (v. 29). The God of Israel had indeed rescued from Nebuchadnezzar's hand these three, who, in themselves, were absolutely powerless. The king's viewpoint did a complete about-face: defiance of the king's command should have brought death; instead defiance brought life (vv. 28-29).

The irony of this story is that what the political enemies of Shadrach, Meshach, and Abednego had plotted was completely overturned. Instead of demotion and death, the three Judean exiles received promotion and prosperity "in the province of Babylon" (v. 30).

"Like a Son of the Gods" (Dan. 3:25)

The New International Version translates Nebuchadnezzar's description of the fourth figure in the blazing furnace (Aramaic, *dāmēh bar 'ĕlāhîn*) as "like a son of the gods." The King James Version translated this phrase as the "Son of God," leading some to see the figure to be a preincarnation appearance of Christ. Jim Edlin observes, however, that "this is likely assuming too much for the context" (vv. 24-25).[8] Yet, when viewed through Nebuchadnezzar's eyes, it is possible that he believed he saw deity—that is, "an actual god," or at least a "divine being."[9] Later, when praising the "God of Shadrach, Meshach and Abednego" for rescuing them, the king identified this fourth figure as "his angel [*mal'ăkēh*]," which can also be translated as "his messenger" (v. 28).

---

7. Ibid., 241.
8. Edlin, *Daniel*, 99.
9. Goldingay, *Daniel*, 235.

Jesus's Raising of Lazarus from the Dead

To one familiar with the New Testament accounts of Jesus's earthly ministry, when reading the account of Shadrach, Meshach, and Abednego coming forth from the blazing furnace, Jesus's calling forth the dead Lazarus at Bethany comes to mind. Standing at the entrance of Lazarus's tomb, among many onlookers, Jesus called out, "Lazarus, come out!" (John 11:43). Lazarus came out, alive, though he was still wrapped in his grave clothes, which Jesus commanded those standing by to remove (v. 44). Both events are events of "resurrection": Shadrach, Meshach, and Abednego were as good as dead and yet lived; Lazarus was indeed dead and yet lived again. John Goldingay observes that what happened in Daniel 3 and other events like it are indications that God is, and always has been, the God who resurrects.[10]

Customs and Practices Explained

Mesopotamian Images (Dan. 3:1)

A. Leo Oppenheim offers the following:

What we know about these [Mesopotamian] images from fragments, representations, and clay replicas is supplemented by literary evidence. We learn that most images were made of precious wood and where not covered with garments were plated with gold; and they had the characteristic staring eyes made of precious stones inset in a naturalistic way and were clad in sumptuous garments of characteristic style, crowned with tiaras and adorned with pectorals.[11]

---

10. Ibid., 242.
11. Oppenheim, *Ancient Mesopotamia*, 184.

Musical Instruments in the Ancient Near East (Dan. 3:5, 10)[12]

Most of our information about the musical instruments used in the ancient Near East come from the Old Testament. Daniel 3:5 (and 10) mentions three kinds of wind instruments (horns, flutes, and pipes) and three kinds of stringed instruments (zithers, lyres, and harps), plus "all kinds of music." This latter catchall phrase may have included percussion instruments. Some of the instruments we know from the Old Testament are as follows.

Wind Instruments

"Flute" or "Pipe" (chalil). This had finger holes, so the player could produce different pitches, thus a melody (1 Kings 1:40; Isa. 30:29; Jer. 48:36).

"Trumpet" (chatsotserah). Made of hammered silver, this horn was straight, used to call the community (Num. 10:1-10), and to accompany praise to the Lord (*yhwh*) (Ezra 3:10; Ps. 98:6). It was also blown when going into battle (Num. 10:9). With no finger holes, this instrument could emit only a few pitches.

"(Ram's) Horn" (qeren). This was a loud trumpetlike instrument, made from the horn of a sheep or goat. It was used in battle situations (Josh. 6:5 [NIV's "trumpets," but not NIV's "trumpets" in v. 4, which is *shophar*, also made from a ram's horn—confusing, I know!]). This horn also could emit only a few pitches.

"Trumpet" or "(Ram's) Horn" (shophar). This is the so-called turned-up horn, also made from the horn of a sheep or goat. It was very loud and piercing and could emit only a limited number of pitches. It was also used in battle (Josh. 6:4 [NIV's "trumpets," but not NIV's "trumpets" of v. 5, which is *qeren*, also made from a ram's horn—confusing, I know!]). It was also blown at coronations (2 Sam. 15:10 [NIV: "trumpets"]) and on special religious events (6:15 [NIV: "trumpets"]).

---

12. Principal source for this section is Scott Aniol, "Music in the Ancient Near East," in *The Lexham Bible Dictionary*, ed. John D. Barry (Bellingham, WA: Lexham Press, 2016), n.p., Logos Bible Software.

"Bagpipe" or "Pipe" (sumphonyah). This may not be a single instrument, but the term may possibly indicate the sound that multiple instruments make when played together, similar to the Greek term *symphōnia*, from which comes the English term *symphony*. The New International Version translates the term "pipe" in Daniel 3:5.

"Pipe" or "Organ" (ugav). This instrument may have been a single pipe or a group of pipes or may have been a type of flute. We hear it on occasions of both joy (Job 21:12; Ps. 150:4) and mourning (Job 30:31).

Stringed Instruments

Six different stringed instruments are mentioned in the Old Testament in use for group worship and political events. These instruments would have been used elsewhere in the ancient Near East as well. The exact meanings of the various terms for these instruments are unclear. The English translations give different English names for the same Hebrew or Aramaic term.

There is no indication that any of these instruments were used with a bow; rather, musical notes were produced by plucking the strings with the fingers. Virtually all of them were portable, though some obviously were smaller, some larger. These are best identified by their Hebrew names, with the New International Version translations: the *qathros* ("zither" [Dan. 3:5]); the *kinnor* ("harp" [1 Sam. 10:5]); the *nevel* ("lyre" [1 Chron. 15:20]); the *pesanterin* ("harp" [Dan. 3:5]); the *sabbekha'* ("lyre" [Dan. 3:5]); and the *asor* ("ten-stringed lyre" [Ps. 33:2]).

God behind the Scenes

God is not mentioned in story three until Daniel 3:17 in the affirmation of Shadrach, Meshach, and Abednego to King Nebuchadnezzar: "the God whom we serve" (AT). This God does not speak to them or reveal to them any dreams or visions. He simply *is*; he *exists*. It is his existence that gives them absolute assurance that whether their life continues in the body or their life is snuffed out in the blazing furnace, they are still and always his servants.

The Story's Relationship, If Any, to the Other Five Stories or Four Visions in Daniel

John Goldingay suggests that Shadrach, Meshach, and Abednego were unwavering in their faithfulness and confidence in God and his ability to deliver them—even from death. Goldingay suggest that this trust and assurance must be understood in the larger context of the book of Daniel—that is, in the awakening of the dead envisioned in Daniel 12:2.[13]

Faithful Living Today

We who live today a life within the context of a commitment to our Lord Jesus Christ have both Jesus's *promise* of eternal resurrection life and the historical resurrection *example* of Jesus himself.

Promise

On the occasion of his raising Lazarus from death to life (but not to eternal resurrection life), Jesus assured Lazarus's sister Martha, "I am the resurrection and the life. The one who believes in me will live, even though they die; and whoever lives by believing in me will never die" (John 11:25-26).

Example

Though killed by his human enemies, Jesus appeared in his resurrection body to his faithful followers (Luke 24:26-49; John 20:19-23, 26-29; 21:1-23) and later ascended into heaven (Luke 24:50-51; see Acts 7:55-56).

We have this witness, then, of both promise and example—of which Shadrach, Meshach, and Abednego had only a glimpse—that can be our anchor in times of crisis that may require our very lives. Faithful living is not only for the duration of our lifetime on this earth but also for the transition into our eternal life hereafter.

---

13. Goldingay, *Daniel*, 242.

9

Story Four (Dan. 4)

Summary

In story four (Dan. 4), the last in which King Nebuchadnezzar appears, the king had a dream of an enormous tree, whose meaning he was at a loss to understand. He called his Babylonian counselors, "but they could not interpret it" (v. 7 [4 HB]). The last to come before the king was Daniel, the "chief of the magicians" (v. 9 [6 HB]), whom Nebuchadnezzar recognized as one in whom God's Spirit (or spirit) was active (vv. 8-9 [5-6 HB]). Daniel did, indeed, interpret the king's dream. The story then unfolds with the outworking of the dream's interpretation in Nebuchadnezzar's life. The story concludes with Nebuchadnezzar recognizing that God is absolutely sovereign over all "the powers of heaven and the peoples of the earth" (v. 35 [32 HB]).

The Story

Story four (Dan. 4) opens with a royal public announcement or proclamation in the name of King Nebuchadnezzar. It was addressed "To the nations and peoples of every language, who live in all the earth" (v. 1 [3:31 HB]). This assumed more than was reality. Though his empire did include peoples of many differing languages, cultures, and ethnicities, Nebuchadnezzar's rule did have geographical boundaries; there were indeed peoples who lived outside Babylon's reach. But such a statement made Nebuchadnezzar appear, at least in his own eyes, more important than any one king really was.

This address is followed by "something of a standard greeting" of ancient Aramaic letters known to scholars today.[1] This greeting includes the Aramaic word *shelam* or *šĕlām* ("peace," "well-being") equivalent to the Hebrew *shalom* or *šālōm* (peace), with which most of us are familiar. The greeting in Nebuchadnezzar's proclamation is "May your peace/well-being increase" (4:1, AT [3:31 HB]).

From Daniel 4:2-18 [3:32–4:15 HB]) Nebuchadnezzar personally speaks. In his opening remarks, Nebuchadnezzar tells his people that the purpose of his proclamation was to inform them of "the wondrous signs that God on High has done for me"[2] (v. 3 [3:33 HB]). He then declared concerning this God that "his kingship lasts through the ages, his rule through all generations!"[3] (v. 3 [3:33 HB]). He made a similar statement about God at the conclusion of his proclamation: "His rule lasts through the ages, his kingship through all generations"[4] (4:34 [v. 31 HB]). Thus Nebuchadnezzar's opening evaluation of the "Most High God" (4:2 [3:32 HB]) is in fact his conclusion after all that is prophesied in his dream has been fulfilled.

All was going well for Nebuchadnezzar, it seemed, "at home in my palace, contented and prosperous" (4:4 [v. 1 HB]). But then the unexpected intruded. One night, while lying on his bed, he *saw* in his head fearful visions and images that greatly terrified him, which he later called a "dream" (*ḥēlem*) (v. 5 [2 HB]; in both Aramaic and Hebrew idiom one *sees* a dream).

What could such a terrifying dream possibly mean, both for him, the king, and for the kingdom? Calling his advisors—"magicians, enchanters, astrologers and diviners"—Nebuchadnezzar told them the details of his dream, expecting an interpretation (v. 7 [4 HB]; see the subsection titled

---

1. Tanner, *Daniel*, 268.
2. Goldingay, *Daniel*, 245.
3. Ibid.
4. Ibid., 247.

"Dreams and Dream Books in Mesopotamia and Egypt," in section titled "Customs and Practices Explained," in ch. 7, "Story Two [Dan. 2]," p. 73). After all, that was one of the duties of their royal employment.

Alas! His advisors were at a loss. The New International Version of 4:7 (v. 4 HB) reads, "They *could not* interpret it for me" (emphasis added). But the Aramaic reads, "Its interpretation they *did not* make known to me" (AT; emphasis added). In verse 18 (15 HB), however, the king told Daniel, "All the wise men of my kingdom *were unable* to make known to me the interpretation" (AT; emphasis added).

So was it *could* not or *would* not? Whichever was the case, the day was saved when Daniel, "chief of the magicians," showed up (4:8-9 [vv. 5-6 HB]).

As chief, why was Daniel last in line? Perhaps he was graciously giving these "lesser diviners" a chance to show their stuff to the king.[5] Or perhaps he wanted to "give time for the deficiency of the other wise men to show itself," he himself stepping in only when their limited skills proved insufficient.[6]

Seemingly as an aside, in his opening introduction, Nebuchadnezzar mentioned to his audience Daniel's Babylonian name, Belteshazzar (v. 8 [5 HB]), which had been given him some years earlier, at the beginning of his conscription for training in the ways of the Babylonian royal court (1:7). This name, noted the king, is like "the name of my god" (4:8 [v. 5 HB]). He was apparently referring to the "Bel" portion of Daniel's Babylonian name, which is another name for Marduk, the chief patron deity of Babylon.

Nebuchadnezzar, moreover, noted concerning Daniel that "the spirit of the holy gods is in him" (v. 8 [5 HB]). Whether or not Nebuchadnezzar had in view Bel (Marduk) and/or other Mesopotamian deities when he said this, one cannot know for sure. Some scholars are reluctant to credit Nebuchadnezzar with referencing Daniel's God of Israel in this statement. For example, Ernest Lucas says, "On Nebuchadnezzar's lips the description of

---

5. Edlin, *Daniel*, 114.
6. Leon J. Wood, *A Commentary on Daniel* (Grand Rapids: Zondervan, 1973; repr., Eugene, OR: Wipf and Stock, 1998), 105.

Daniel's source of insight . . . is most naturally taken in a polytheistic sense."[7] John Goldingay, however, notes that the king perceives the spirit of God in Daniel.[8]

Earlier, concerning Nebuchadnezzar's dream experience of Daniel 2, the king's experts had told the king that mysteries such as his dreams represented could not be solved except by the gods, and since they do not dwell among human beings, these resolutions could not be revealed to the king (v. 11). They were right, of course, from their viewpoint and experience. But then Daniel had shown the king that "there is a God in heaven who reveals mysteries" (v. 28). He then proceeded to reveal the mystery of *that* dream to King Nebuchadnezzar. The king recognized that it was Daniel's God and Daniel working in tandem that enabled Daniel to reveal the dream's mystery (v. 47).

So, we cannot divorce story four (Dan. 4) from story two (Dan. 2), as though King Nebuchadnezzar had learned nothing of the God of heaven through his first dream experience and Daniel's interpretation of it. It was now to *Daniel* that he expressed confidence that "no mystery is too difficult for you" and that this was so because "I know that the spirit of the holy gods is in you" (4:9 [v. 6 HB]).

The main details of his dream that King Nebuchadnezzar told to Daniel are as follows (vv. 10-17 [7-14 HB]):

The king saw a large tree growing in the middle of the earth, whose top touched the heavens. It was so large it could be seen from everywhere on the earth. Wild animals sheltered under it, birds made its branches home, and it provided food for creatures of every kind (vv. 10-12 [7-9 HB]).

As Nebuchadnezzar was observing this large tree in his dream, his eyes were drawn toward the heavens, from which he saw descending a being whom he called "a watcher" (AT) and "a holy one" (see subsection titled "The Heavenly Watcher [Dan. 4:13 (v. 10 HB)]," in section titled "Customs and Practices Explained," pp. 98-99).

---

7. Lucas, *Daniel*, 109.
8. Goldingay, *Daniel*, 258.

The New International Version describes this figure as "a messenger" (v. 23 [20 HB]). This messenger had a message, given "in the form of a royal proclamation,"[9] sent on behalf of "the Most High" (see v. 24 [21 HB]). Paradoxically, this message, addressed to no one in particular, in fact, was addressed to all (v. 13 [10 HB]). The message was that Nebuchadnezzar's dream tree was to be cut down, its branches lopped off, its leaves stripped, and its fruit scattered. No longer were the animals and birds to enjoy the tree's sanctuary and protection (vv. 14-15a [11-12a HB]).

The Aramaic language does not have the neuter gender pronoun "it" or "its." Therefore, the masculine singular pronoun "him" or "his" is also used for "it" or "its." Thus, when the messenger says in verse 15a (12a HB) "But leave in the earth the stock of *its* root" (AT; emphasis added), he is using the pronoun with the double meaning of both "its" and "his," thus pointing to the human figure that is the focus of verse 15b (12b HB): "the stock of *his* root" (AT; emphasis added). Looking ahead to Daniel's interpretation of the dream, we will see that God is leaving the "root" of Nebuchadnezzar's kingdom in the land, to be restored to him again after his recovery from his dementia (see v. 26 [23 HB]).

The "ring of iron and bronze"[10] mentioned in verse 15a (12a HB) most likely refers to a fetter or tether controlling the demented man we see in the description in verse 16 (13 HB): wetted with heaven's dew, eating wild herbage with the animals, his mind reduced to an animallike state. That the "ring of iron and bronze" refers to a tether for controlling a demented person "to keep them from destroying themselves or attacking others with weapons" was the church father Jerome's interpretation as early as the fifth century AD.[11]

The heavenly watcher then declared that other heavenly "watchers" (AT [NIV: "messengers"]) or "holy ones" concurred in the "decision" or "verdict"

---

9. Edlin, *Daniel*, 114.
10. Goldingay, *Daniel*, 246.
11. Gleason L. Archer Jr., trans., *Jerome's Commentary on Daniel* (Grand Rapids: Baker, 1958), 50-51.

that is now being announced from heaven; they spoke with one voice on behalf of "the Most High" (v. 17 [14 HB]). The announcement was not only for King Nebuchadnezzar but also for "the living"—that is, for all human beings (v. 17 [14 HB]).

The announcement was that "the Most High rules over human kingship, and to whomever he wishes he gives it; even the lowliest of persons he may set over it" (v. 17 [14 HB], AT). God's capacity to take power from the powerful and bestow it on the powerless was not simply a theological hope of Israel's prophets. This truth was demonstrated in the present time of Daniel's life: God ended Nebuchadnezzar's rule and gave its authority to a nobody successor like Nabonidus.[12]

After telling Daniel the details of his dream, King Nebuchadnezzar requested of Daniel, "Tell me what it means" (v. 18 [15 HB]). The king had already asked the wise men in his employ to interpret the dream, but they were unable. The king was sure Daniel could do so, "Because," he said, "the spirit of the holy gods is in you" (v. 18 [15 HB]) (see comments on v. 8 [5 HB], pp. 90-91).

Daniel understood the meaning of the dream immediately, and that understanding gave him considerable terror. Why? His terror came from his desire not to have to tell the king what the dream meant. Goldingay suggests that Daniel did not relish conveying words of judgment.[13] So, to soften the word of judgment that he must inevitably reveal to the king, he first expressed his wish that the king's enemies might be the recipients of the dream's meaning. But he could not delay long, for the king was anxious to know the dream's meaning (v. 19 [16 HB]).

So, with no beating around the bush, Daniel gave King Nebuchadnezzar the dream's "interpretation" and God's "decree," followed by a word of personal "advice" (vv. 24, 27 [21, 24 HB]).

12. Goldingay, *Daniel*, 267.
13. Ibid., 268.

The *interpretation* was that King Nebuchadnezzar, himself, was the large, strong, life-giving tree (vv. 20-23 [17-20 HB]).

The *decree*, issued from the Most High (God) himself, was (1) that King Nebuchadnezzar would be driven away from humanity for a period of time, implying a temporary removal from his position as ruler of Babylon; (2) that during this time of removal he would live among the wild animals, eating plants like an ox, drenched daily with heaven's dew; (3) that he would remain in this state until he came to acknowledge that the Most High is absolute ruler over human kingship; and (4) that the tree's root stock that was left in the ground represented Nebuchadnezzar's kingship and, as such, would be reconfirmed or restored to him when he has acknowledged that Heaven (= the Most High) is the absolute ruler (vv. 25-26 [22-23 HB]).

Daniel's *advice* to King Nebuchadnezzar was that he should "atone for" (NRSV) or "redeem" or "make amends for"[14] his sins through acts of righteousness, and his iniquities through acts of kindness to the poor (v. 27 [24 HB]). If the king were to assume this new style of rule, his people would see him, in the right sense, as an emperor with new clothes, to be compared with Old Testament Job, wearing righteousness for his clothing and justice for his robe and turban (see Job 29:14). Ironically, in the opening lines of his building inscription number 12, Nebuchadnezzar casts himself as "the just king, meek and humble, . . . lover of faithfulness and justice, regardful of life."[15] Thus, if the king were, indeed, to practice in his rule what he claimed of himself, as Daniel urged, then, added Daniel, "It may be that then your prosperity will continue" (Dan. 4:27 [v. 24 HB]).

What was King Nebuchadnezzar's response to Daniel's interpretation of his dream? Did he believe that what God had decreed would *really* happen to him? The implication seems to be that he simply shrugged his shoulders and went on with his life as usual.

---

14. *Theologic al Dictionary of the Old Testament: Vol. 16, Aramaic Dictionary*, ed. Holger Gzella, trans. Mark E. Biddle (Grand Rapids: Eerdmans, 2018), 612, Oaktree Software/Accordance.

15. Stephen Langdon, *Building Inscriptions of the Neo-Babylonian Empire: Part 1, Nabopolassar and Nebuchadnezzar* (Paris: Ernest Leroux, 1905), 97.

Twelve months pass with no mention of either Daniel or King Nebuchadnezzar. At the end of these twelve months the narrator captures well Nebuchadnezzar's pride while one day out strolling on the roof of his Babylonian palace. As he scanned the length and breadth of the city, perhaps with arms stretched wide, the king called out, no doubt to his servants who surely would have been attending him, "Is not this the great Babylon *I* have built as the royal residence, by *my* mighty power and for the glory of *my* majesty?" (v. 30 [27 HB]; emphasis added).

The narrator then makes a wordplay: While Nebuchadnezzar's prideful "*words* were still in his mouth, a *voice* fell from the heavens" (v. 31 [28 HB], AT; emphasis added)—voice against voice, the voice of the heavenly King overruled the voice of Babylon's earthly king. The words of this heavenly voice were indeed chilling: Daniel's interpretation of the king's dream of twelve months earlier was about to be fulfilled (vv. 31-32 [28-29 HB]).

The narrator says, "Immediately" (v. 33 [30 HB]). Everything in life that King Nebuchadnezzar had going for him collapsed with a suddenness that left him totally confused and bereft of all personal control: driven away from the companionship of fellow humans; access to none of the delicious royal foods when he hungered, but eating plants and grasses with the oxen in the fields; sleeping in the open, his body and clothing daily soaked with the dew of the night; and deprived of his royal barber and manicurist (v. 33 [30 HB]).

The story now resumes in King Nebuchadnezzar's voice. He testifies that he "raised [his] eyes toward heaven" (v. 34 [31 HB]). These "words form the turning point of the story"; they signify that King Nebuchadnezzar turned to God Most High in faith and trust (cf. Pss. 121:1; 123:1-2).[16] The Aramaic phrase that the New International Version translates "My sanity was restored" (v. 34 [31 HB]) expresses more specifically, "My intellectual capacity of recognition returned to me."[17] Though the king's level of faith was basic and undeveloped, it was from this faith that he could now praise,

---

16. Edlin, *Daniel*, 121.
17. See *Theological Dictionary of the Old Testament: Vol. 16*, 338.

honor, and glorify God Most High and declare that God "lives forever" (v. 34 [31 HB]). J. Paul Tanner says, "We may well assume that Nebuchadnezzar himself became a true believer in the same God as Daniel and will one day stand with Daniel in the kingdom of God that will be given to the son of Man"[18] (v. 34a [31a HB]).

What might Nebuchadnezzar have meant when he declared that God "lives forever"? Informative is his added affirmation that God's "kingdom endures from generation to generation" and that "all the inhabitants [NIV: "peoples"] of the earth are accounted as not [kālâ; NIV: "as nothing"]" (vv. 34-35 [31-32 HB], AT). The Aramaic terms for "generation" and "inhabitants" are from the same root (dwr).[19] Thus earth's inhabitants are viewed here in terms of generational time measurements: one generation comes to an end and is "accounted as not"—that is, no longer existing, giving its place to another generation. God and his kingdom, however, is nongenerational, never passing away, continuing on throughout and beyond all generations of earth's inhabitants. Nebuchadnezzar, moreover, acknowledged that God Most High is absolutely sovereign over *both* "the host of heaven [ḥêl šĕmayyā'] and the inhabitants of the earth" (v. 35 [32 HB], AT). Neither the heavenly nor the earthly beings created by God, Nebuchadnezzar averred, may challenge anything that God chooses to do: "He does as he pleases" (v. 35 [32 HB]).

King Nebuchadnezzar then testified that with the return of his reasoning ability, he again was given majesty, splendor, and the honor of his kingship. Advisors (an Aramaic word "apparently denot[ing] functionaries from the king's inner circle")[20] and nobles again sought him out. His rehabilitation was to such an extent that he said, "I . . . became even greater than before" (v. 36 [33 HB]). Tanner suggests that "this seems reminiscent of Job's

---

18. Tanner, *Daniel*, 311.
19. *Theological Dictionary of the Old Testament: Vol. 16*, 196.
20. Ibid., 839.

experience."[21] The narrator of Job said, "The LORD blessed the latter part of Job's life more than the former part" (Job 42:12).

King Nebuchadnezzar's final words in story four (Dan. 4)—which at first appear to be words of self-praise—turn to praise of God. It appears that he credits his own becoming "greater than before" to the action of the "King of heaven," whom he praises, exalts, and glorifies "because everything he does is right and all his ways are just" (vv. 36-37 [33-34 HB]). And no doubt referring to himself as one who used to "walk in pride," Nebuchadnezzar has been humbled by this Supreme King (v. 37 [34 HB]).

Customs and Practices Explained

The Title "King of the World" (Dan. 4:1 [3:31 HB])

Sumerian legend believed that after the flood, kingship descended from heaven to humans in the Sumerian city of Kish. Enlil, the principal deity of the pantheon of gods, was the source of this kingship. A human king who ruled from Kish was suzerain of the whole world!

The Akkadian title *šar-kiššati*, meaning "King of Kish" and, by extension, "King of the World," was first taken by Sargon I in ca. 2330 BC. He rose to power in the city of Kish and then extended his rule over all Sumer and perhaps to the northern regions of Mesopotamia. He later moved his royal residence to the city of Akkad, near the later city of Babylon.[22]

A thousand years later, *Assyrian* kings, extending their rule from the city of Nineveh in Mesopotamia, southward to Babylon and westward to the Mediterranean Sea, reapplied to themselves Sargon's title, "King of the World." Some of these, for example, were Tiglath-Pileser I (r. 1114–1076 BC), Shalmaneser III (r. 858-824 BC), Adad-Nirari III (r. 810–783 BC),

21. Tanner, *Daniel*, 312.

22. John Bright, *History of Israel*, 36; Yigal Levin, "Nimrod the Mighty, King of Kish, King of Sumer and Akkad," *Vetus Testamentum* 52, no. 3 (2002): 362; Joan Oates, *Babylon* (London: Thames and Hudson, 1979), 27-28; Kathryn Stevens, "The Antiochus Cylinder, Babylonian Scholarship and Seleucid Imperial Ideology," *Journal of Hellenic Studies* 134 (2014): 73; *Ancient Near Eastern Texts*, 267.

Sennacherib (r. 704–681 BC), Esarhaddon (r. 680-669 BC), and Ashurba-nipal (r. 668-633 BC).[23]

The *Babylonian* kings, ruling from the city of Babylon, took over all the former Assyrian Empire's territory and more. They generally did not use the title "King of the World," though it was "used of Nabopolassar and Nebuchadnezzar II in economic documents and a colophon, but not in royal inscriptions."[24] Perhaps in his announcement, however, Nebuchadnezzar's use of the words "To the nations and peoples of every language, who live in *all the earth*" (Dan. 4:1; emphasis added) is a camouflaged attempt to *apply* this historic title without actually using it.

Allegiance to the Deity Bel (Marduk) (Dan. 4:8 [v. 5 HB]: *Bel*teshazzar)

Nebuchadnezzar pointedly addressed Daniel by his Babylonian name, Belteshazzar (here, with an Aramaic spelling). This name is equivalent to the Assyrian-Babylonian name *Bēl-šar-uṣur*, meaning "O Bel, protect the king."[25] Jim Edlin suggests, "Perhaps repetition of the name offers some comfort to a troubled king."[26]

The patron deity of the city of Babylon was Bel. But in his historical documents, King Nebuchadnezzar referred to Bel by his other name, Marduk. For example, "(Two lines destroyed) [from] the Upper Sea [to] the Lower Sea (one line destroyed) . . . which Marduk my lord, has entrusted to me, I have made . . . the city of Babylon to the foremost among all the countries and every human habitation."[27]

The Heavenly Watcher (Dan. 4:13 [v. 10 HB])

Nebuchadnezzar speaks of a figure "descending from heaven" (4:13, AT). Then he describes this figure with the Aramaic phrase *'îr wĕqaddîš*—that is,

23. *Ancient Near Eastern Texts*, 274, 276, 281, 288-89, 297.
24. Stevens, "Antiochus Cylinder," 73, n. 32.
25. Knut L. Tallqvist, *Assyrian Personal Names* (Helsingfors, FIN: Societas Scientiarum Fennica, 1914), 61b, Google Books.
26. Edlin, *Daniel*, 113.
27. *Ancient Near Eastern Texts*, 307.

"an *'îr*, indeed, a holy one." Now, what is an *'îr*? The New International Version translates the term as "a messenger." This is not wrong. The Aramaic term *'îr*, however, contains the concept of one who is "watchful" or "wakeful";[28] thus several English versions prefer the term "watcher" (ESV, NJPS, NKJV, NRSV, NASB), while John Goldingay translates the term as "lookout."[29]

These "lookouts" or "watchmen" appear elsewhere in the Old Testament, identified by various terms. In Isaiah 62:6, they appear as God-appointed "watchmen" (*šōměrîm*) on Jerusalem's walls, "whose sole task is not to allow [God] to forget how precious Jerusalem . . . is to him and what he has promised to do for it."[30] In 1 Kings 22:19-22, they appear as the "host of heaven" (*ṣěbā' haššāmayim*), of whom one was a "deceiving spirit" (*rûaḥ šeqer*). In Job 1:6 and 2:1, those gathered before Yahweh are "the sons of God" (*běnê hā'ělōhîm*), of whom one is called "Satan" or "the adversary."[31] In Psalm 89:5-7 (vv. 6-8 HB), they appear as "the assembly of the holy ones" (*qěhal qědōšîm*), "the sons of the mighty" (AT; *běnê 'ēlîm*), and "the council of the holy ones" (*sôd qědōšîm*).

God behind the Scenes

Throughout the entirety of story four (Dan. 4) we see God's silent influence on King Nebuchadnezzar's heart and mind. His recognition that God "the Most High" is absolutely sovereign in the affairs of both heaven and earth is the *main point* of the story (vv. 17, 32 [14, 29 HB]). This recognition also forms the *envelope* or *inclusio* in which the story is told (vv. 2-3 [3:32-33 HB]; 4:34-35 [vv. 31-32 HB]).

---

28. F. Brown, S. R. Driver, and C. A. Briggs, *A Hebrew and English Lexicon of the Old Testament* (Oxford, UK: Oxford University Press, 1907), 1105; *Theological Dictionary of the Old Testament: Vol. 16*, 565.

29. Goldingay, *Daniel*, 245.

30. Oswalt, *Book of Isaiah*, 584.

31. *Dictionary of Classical Hebrew*, 8:123.

The Story's Relationship, If Any, to the Other Five Stories or Four Visions in Daniel

Story four (Dan. 4), which features King Nebuchadnezzar, has a close relationship with story five (Dan. 5), which features King Belshazzar. John Goldingay, commenting on Daniel 5, notes that because Belshazzar failed to gain insight from what happened to Nebuchadnezzar, he would suffer severer consequences for his blasphemous behavior.[32] Shane Kirkpatrick explains further:

Daniel 4 is the positive example of an earthly king [Nebuchadnezzar] who suffers a great indignity and thereby comes to "know" that God has sovereignty over human kingship, whereupon the king has his earthly dominion restored to him. Daniel 5 is the negative example of an earthly king [Belshazzar] who has not learned the lesson, does not acknowledge God's sovereignty, and thereby suffers the ultimate loss of not only his kingship but also his life.[33]

Faithful Living Today

In story four (Dan. 4), when King Nebuchadnezzar "commanded that all the wise men of Babylon be brought before" him to give him an interpretation of his dream (v. 6 [3 HB]), because of his rank as "chief of the magicians" (v. 9 [6 HB]), Daniel would have been among them. Because of his rank, he certainly could have spoken first. Yet we find Daniel waiting in the wings, allowing the other advisors to try their hand at pleasing the king with their interpretations. Only when it became evident that they hadn't a clue about the significance of the dream did Daniel step forward to be recognized by the king as one in whom God's Spirit resided (v. 8 [5 HB]).

This is the kind of faithful living to which we are called today. We do not always need to be first and foremost with our words and opinions. We

32. Goldingay, *Daniel*, 257.

33. Shane Kirkpatrick, *Competing for Honor: A Social-Scientific Reading of Daniel 1–6* (Leiden, NL: Brill, 2005), 118, EBSCOhost.

must wait for God's Spirit to prompt us when to speak or for another to recognize God's Spirit within us.

10

Story Five (Dan. 5)

Summary

Story five (Dan. 5) accounts for only a single night in the life of arrogant, blasphemous Babylonian king Belshazzar. Ancient Mesopotamian records indicate that the events of this night fell on October 12, 539 BC.[1] In this night, Belshazzar unexpectedly encountered God's prophet Daniel while he (the king) was throwing a sumptuous banquet for at least a thousand guests (v. 1).

Who Was Belshazzar?

The narrator three times names Nebuchadnezzar as Belshazzar's "father" (Dan. 5:2, 11, 13), yet data from Mesopotamian cuneiform texts have made clear that Belshazzar was the son of King Nabonidus.[2] For a brief discussion of the identity of Belshazzar, see the first paragraph of the section titled "The Fifth Story (Dan. 5)," in chapter 4, "Chapter Summaries," page 30.

---

1. Edlin, *Daniel*, 141.
2. Goldingay, *Daniel*, 288.

During this banquet, Belshazzar ordered "cultic vessels"[3] that had been confiscated from God's Jerusalem temple be brought from storage to the banquet so that he and his guests might drink wine from them (vv. 2-3). Then, while he and his guests drank from them, in blasphemous arrogance, they praised their "gods of gold and silver, of bronze, iron, wood and stone" (v. 4).

Suddenly, mysterious "fingers of a human hand" (v. 5) appeared, writing words on the wall of the banquet hall. The "enchanters, astrologers and diviners" in the king's employ were summoned to explain this phenomenon, but they hadn't a clue (vv. 7-8). So Daniel was called, and through the inspiration of the Most High God, he both read the writing and gave its interpretation (vv. 13-28).

Story five (Dan. 5) concludes abruptly. In that very night of drunken carousing, Darius the Mede captured Babylon, and King Belshazzar was killed (v. 30). This happened in 539 BC, ending Babylonian rule of the biblical world and marking the beginning of Persian rule.

The Story

Story five (Dan. 5) opens in Babylon at the banquet hall of Babylonian king Belshazzar, where he is throwing a lavish banquet. The king's banquet hall must have been huge, for "his thousand nobles" (v. 1, AT) had been invited to the gala celebration.

The Babylonian Throne Room

German archaeologist Robert Koldewey directed the excavation of the ancient city of Babylon (in modern-day Iraq), with some two hundred workers laboring daily year-round from 1899 through 1914. Of the many rooms of Nebuchadnezzar's palace that Koldewey unearthed, "the largest chamber of the Citadel" he believed to be "the throne-room of the Babylonian kings." Of this, he wrote,

---

3. *Theological Dictionary of the Old Testament: Vol. 16*, 399.

It is so clearly marked out for this purpose that no reasonable doubt can be felt as to its having been used as their principal audience chamber. If any one should desire to localise the scene of Belshazzar's eventful banquet, he can surely place it with complete accuracy in this immense room. It is 17 meters broad and 52 meters long [approx. 56 by 171 ft.]. . . . Immediately opposite the main door in the back wall there is a doubly recessed niche in which doubtless the throne stood, so that the king could be visible to those who stood in the court.[4]

What the king was celebrating the narrator does not say. Was it "hubris," a term that speaks of pride beyond pride, of arrogance and empty self-importance? Why was he throwing this big party when, in light of verse 30, the Median-Persian army was at his very gates? Was the king flaunting a "don't give a rip" attitude before his guests, or was he just plain stupid?

As a kind of an aside, the narrator mentions some "extras" in attendance at this extravaganza—the king's "wives" and "concubines" (v. 2). These were at his beck and call to satisfy his every sexual desire. They were in a class well below the status of the "queen" (v. 10), who may have been Belshazzar's main *wife*, although she may have been a queen mother, but which king's mother cannot be determined.[5] In any case, the queen had absented herself from the wine drinking revelry, as perhaps her status deemed her above such frivolity.

The story moves quickly to Belshazzar's open and defiant act of blasphemy against the God of the universe, who has been present behind the scenes throughout the previous four stories. No doubt somewhat drunk—for the narrator commented, "while he was drinking wine" (v. 2, AT)—Belshazzar suddenly recalled that the former Babylonian king, Nebuchadnezzar, had brought to Babylon sacred cultic vessels that he had earlier confiscated from the Jerusalem temple. These cultic vessels belonged to the God of the

---

4. Robert Koldewey, *The Excavations at Babylon*, trans. Agnes S. Johns (London: Macmillan, 1914), 103-4, Internet Archive.

5. *Theological Dictionary of the Old Testament: Vol. 16*, 764.

universe, who claimed that temple as his earthly home. Nebuchadnezzar had put these cultic vessels in Babylon's royal treasury, where they had been kept safe since that time. But now, what better way to impress Belshazzar's thousand guests and his female lovers with his importance than to drink wine from some of these sacred vessels? After all, *he*, the king, had neither fear of nor reverence for this foreign God. Thus Belshazzar ordered that "the gold and silver vessels" (AT) be brought to the banquet hall (v. 2).

Aramaic *mā'n* (Cultic Vessel)

The Aramaic term *mā'n* (cultic vessel) does not specifically refer to vessels in the shape of "goblets," as the New International Version interpretively indicates (Dan. 5:2, 3), but to vessels "of any type, of whatever size, composition, and value."[6] Gold and silver vessels had been confiscated from the Jerusalem temple and kept in storage in Babylon for many years. When the first batch of exiles returned to Judea in 539 BC, they carried them back to Jerusalem for the temple they were planning to rebuild. Before departing, one of the exiles made an inventory of these "cultic vessels": a total of 5,400! Of these, vessels from which Belshazzar and his guests might have drunk wine the night of Babylon's fall were 1,030 gold and silver "dishes" and 440 gold and silver "bowls" (Ezra 1:9-11).

Belshazzar and his guests' drinking from these sacred vessels was blasphemous enough. But as they were drinking the wine, in an act of bravado to show their contempt for the living God, he and his lovers raised their voices in praise to their lifeless, pagan Babylonian gods, which the narrator derisively dismisses as simply "gods of gold and silver, of bronze, iron, wood and stone" (Dan. 5:3-4).

Belshazzar's bravado quickly faded, however, when something phenomenal occurred right in front of the king and presumably his guests. The phenomenon that nearly paralyzed Belshazzar was the appearance of

---

6. Ibid., 398.

a disembodied human hand, its fingers writing on a plastered wall near the light of a lampstand. The narrator, at this point, does not reveal the words that the fingers wrote. It seems that he wants to keep us, his readers, in suspense until an interpreter himself will reveal the words (see v. 25). The narrator rather graphically describes the effect of this phenomenon on Belshazzar: "The king! His face turned pale [lit. "changed"], his thoughts were horrified, his hip joints [lit. "the knots of his hip/loin"] were loosened, and his knees were knocking together!" (vv. 5-6, AT).

Belshazzar immediately called for his "enchanters, astrologers and diviners" (v. 7). To the one among them who could read the writing and declare its interpretation, the king promised to robe him in royal purple, drape his neck with a gold collar (hammôněkā', a Persian loanword indicating a "golden neck ornament"),[7] and elevate him to a high political rank in the Babylonian kingdom (v. 7).

But all the king's advisors, here called "wise men," were clueless. They could neither read the words written on the wall nor interpret their meaning. This terrified Belshazzar even more (vv. 8-9).

The stage was set for the entrance of the queen (mother?), whose apparent "political"[8] status allows her to enter the king's presence without his approval (unlike Esther, the queen of the Persian king Xerxes [Esther 4:11]). Respectfully addressing the king, "O King, live forever" (AT), the queen urged Belshazzar to cool it, relax, no need for alarm (Dan. 5:10). She reminded the king of "a man in your kingdom," whom, in an earlier time, King Nebuchadnezzar had appointed as "chief" over all these clueless wise men or advisors. His name, she said, is Daniel (Belteshazzar).

According to the queen, Daniel's qualifications for doing what Belshazzar needed and wanted were spectacular, seemingly more than one could expect in any one person. The queen got it right, though, when, in verse 11, she mentioned Daniel's primary qualification: he is one "in whom is

---

7. Ibid., 1860.
8. Goldingay, *Daniel*, 289.

the Spirit of the Holy God" (NKJV). She also mentioned additional qualifications in both verses 11 and 12. Some of these are (1) "insight" (nahîrû):
"divine illumination into a matter";[9] (2) "intelligence" (śāklĕṯānû): "prudent
speech and actions as well as intellectual competence";[10] (3) "wisdom" (ḥok-
mā): "applying the right truth at the right time in the right circumstance";[11]
(4) "knowledge" (manda'): this "included awareness gained from personal
experience";[12] and (5) "a solver of enigmas, puzzles, or difficult tasks" (qiṭrîn)
(AT [lit. "of knots";[13] thus "a loosener of knots"]). Of this qualification, Jim
Edlin comments, "When Daniel 'loosens the knots' of the writing on the
wall he will likely further 'loosen the knots' of the king's body"[14] (see comment on Dan. 5:6, pp. 105-6).

The queen then advised Belshazzar to call for Daniel, declaring him to
be the one who can interpret the writing on the wall (v. 12).

Belshazzar listened to the queen, but when Daniel came, the king, in
a royal put-down, sneeringly reminded Daniel of his status as a lowly conscript: "So then, you are Daniel, one of the *exiles* of Judah. I've heard about
you. [They say] that the spirit of deity is in you, and [they say] that illumination, insight, and exceeding wisdom has been found in you" (vv. 13-14, AT;
emphasis added).

The king then admitted to Daniel that his own gaggle of experts were
utter failures; they couldn't explain the writing on the wall (v. 15). Again he
said, "I have heard about you. [They say] that you are able to give interpretations and to solve enigmas or puzzles [lit. "to loosen knots"]" (v. 16, AT).
He then added, with this proviso, "*If you are able* to read aloud [qĕrā']"[15]
the writing and its interpretation to make known to me . . ." (v. 16, AT;
emphasis added). The king's words, "If you can," might imply doubt that this

---

9. Edlin, *Daniel*, 135.
10. Ibid.
11. Ibid.
12. Ibid., 136.
13. *Theological Dictionary of the Old Testament: Vol. 16*, 669.
14. Edlin, *Daniel*, 136.
15. *Theological Dictionary of the Old Testament: Vol. 16*, 675.

lowly exile from Judah could possibly do what his own gaggle of Babylonian experts could not do. Nevertheless, *if* Daniel is successful, then he, the magnanimous king, will award him the jackpot: the purple robe, the gold collar, and promotion to high political office (v. 16).

In verses 17-28, the narrator records Daniel's response to Belshazzar. Daniel rose to the challenge of the king's put-down. "He dispenses with polite protocol and unleashes a prophetic tirade on Belshazzar," observes Jim Edlin.[16]

It was as God's prophet that Daniel confronted Belshazzar, wasting no time on small talk or niceties. Cutting to the chase, and not even giving the king any royal address, Daniel refused Belshazzar's offer of gifts. "Your gifts, keep them for yourself! Your rewards, to another give!" (v. 17, AT).

The New International Version puts a nice spin on Daniel's next words, having him respectfully saying, "Your Majesty." But Daniel's opener is a hammer blow: "*You*, O King" (v. 18, AT; emphasis added). The words that then poured from Daniel's mouth presented former King Nebuchadnezzar (whom Daniel called Belshazzar's father [v. 18]) as the example whom Belshazzar should have emulated. *He*, Nebuchadnezzar, was truly a great king, Daniel implied. Though he had allowed arrogance and pride to harden his heart (v. 20), when the Most High God humbled him, Nebuchadnezzar acknowledged the sovereignty of the Most High God, a sovereignty that extended over all earth's kingdoms (v. 21).

Then came the hammer blow again. The Aramaic word order is important: "But *you*, his son, Belshazzar!" (v. 22, AT; emphasis added). As Nebuchadnezzar's *son*, "*all this* you knew" (v 22, AT; emphasis added). You should have followed his example. But in your arrogance, "you have exalted yourself against the Lord of heaven" (v. 23, AT). Moreover, this Lord of heaven is the "God who has *in his hand* [*bydh*] your life-breath [*nšmtk*] and your fate [*kl 'rḥtk*] [lit. "all your ways"]" (AT; emphasis added).[17] This God "you did

---

16. Edlin, *Daniel*, 137.
17. *Theological Dictionary of the Old Testament: Vol. 16*, 506-7.

not honor. So then, from his presence was sent *the hand* [*yd'*] by which this writing was inscribed" (vv. 23-24, AT; emphasis added). Note the interplay on God's *hand*. Jim Edlin observes, "A hand that announces death through an inscription on a wall (v 24) comes from the hand that holds Belshazzar's life in it (v 23)."[18]

Daniel now both read the cryptically written words on Belshazzar's throne wall and gave an interpretation. We do not know in what script the words on the wall were written. They may have been written in Babylonian cuneiform or in the simpler Aramaic alphabetic letters. In the book of Daniel we have the words written in the Aramaic script. And though they are written in present-day biblical manuscripts with vowel letters, in Daniel's time, if written in Aramaic, they would have been written with consonants only (see the sidebar "Hebrew and Aramaic Vowel Points" below).

Hebrew and Aramaic Vowel Points

Only the consonants of the Hebrew and Aramaic words were written in the oldest manuscripts of the Old Testament, since only an alphabetic system of consonants had been developed. That is, no system of marks or letters to indicate vowels had yet been developed. Readers of the text had to "know" or remember how each cluster of consonants was actually pronounced. The correct pronunciation of the sacred text was passed on from one generation to the next.

Lest the correct pronunciation be forgotten, from the seventh to the eleventh century AD, Jewish rabbis, known as Masoretes, in the cities of Tiberias and Jerusalem, and also in Babylonia, developed a system of "points" for both Hebrew and Aramaic scripts of the biblical consonantal texts. They inserted these "points" above, below, and between the consonants of the original text, each representing a different vowel sound. When read together, these "points" and consonants indicate how the words are to be pronounced.

---

18. Edlin, *Daniel*, 140.

There really wasn't much for Daniel to read, an inscription consisting of four terms only. "Through [this] mysterious inscription, interpreted by Daniel, God announces that he has *determined* to bring an end to the Babylonian monarch's rule and kingdom."[19]

The *first* term, repeated twice, was "MENE, MENE" (v. 25). Daniel understood it to be related to the three-consonant verb *m-n-'* (the third symbol, ', indicates the Hebrew letter aleph), meaning to "number" or "count." He then applied this meaning to Belshazzar's soon to be terminated rule: "God [lit. "the God," implying "the God of the universe, whom you have mocked and dishonored"] has numbered your kingship and has completed or terminated it" (v. 26, AT).

The *second* term was "TEKEL." Daniel understood it to be related to the three-consonant verb *t-k-l*, meaning to "weigh." Thus Daniel interprets, "You [Belshazzar] have been weighed on the balance scale and have been found light or lacking" (v. 27, AT). Jim Edlin suggests that Belshazzar has not weighed up to God's expectations and that it was Nebuchadnezzar who was figuratively placed on the other side of the balance scale, Nebuchadnezzar who had humbled himself and had acknowledged the sovereignty of the Most High God.[20]

The *third* term was "PARSIN." Daniel understood it to be related to the three-consonant verb *p-r-s*, meaning to "divide." Here, Daniel interpreted the term to mean to "break off" or "bring to an end" (v. 28, AT). The consonants *p-r-s* are also the same as the three consonants in the name Persia, *p-r-s*. So this third term may also have alluded to Persia, to whom God was about to hand over rule of the Babylonian kingdom. Median and Persian kings will receive the kingship. The terms "Medes" and "Persians" are often associated together and historically are the two dominant groups of the Persian Empire, which succeeds the Babylonian Empire (v. 28).

---

19. *New International Dictionary of Old Testament*, 2:965; emphasis original.
20. Edlin, *Daniel*, 141.

Jim Edlin's summary of this encounter between King Belshazzar and the prophet Daniel is apt: "The God who supplied Nebuchadnezzar's splendor is ending the deal with the Babylonian kingdom. The message . . . is one of imminent judgment for Belshazzar and the Babylonians. In short, time is up, the verdict is reached, and the sentence awaits execution."[21]

The narrator does not record either Belshazzar's emotional or verbal response to Daniel's explanation of the writing on the wall. But Belshazzar immediately awarded Daniel with the promised purple clothing, gold neck collar, and high political office (v. 29). And, though Daniel had at the beginning of this encounter rejected these rewards, the narrator does not indicate that he now refused them.

Nothing is recorded that indicates that King Belshazzar in any sense understood the import of Daniel's interpretation of the writing on the wall. He gave no acknowledgment of even the existence of God Most High, let alone of God's universal sovereignty, as King Nebuchadnezzar before him had done (see Dan. 4:2-3, 37 [3:32-33; 4:34 HB]). But why would we expect him to do so? This is a story of a monarch who had mocked the living God by desecrating God's sacred temple vessels, while praising his own lifeless Babylonian gods. He treated Daniel's God as though he were as powerless as his own gods! One is reminded of an Israelite prophet's taunt of Babylon's gods on the eve of the Babylonian Empire's handover to Persian Darius-Cyrus, as recorded in Isaiah 41:21-24. B. Ross summarizes the powerlessness of these deities as follows:

> The issue here is the ability [of these deities] to both predict events and to bring them about as predicted. [The prophet] becomes sarcastic. These deities cannot tell us about the future. Can they tell us about the past? No? Can they do something good, or bad? No? Well, then, can they say "Boo" and scare us? The overwhelming answer to these questions is: they are "nothing" and their "work is nothing at all" (NRSV).[22]

21. Ibid.
22. Barry Ross, *Our Incomparable God: A Commentary on Isaiah 40–55* (Pune, IND: Fountain Press, 2003), 38.

The abruptness with which the narrator ends this story of King Belshazzar itself expresses the utter surprise and swiftness with which the end came for the king and Babylon's world rule: "That very night Belshazzar the Babylonian [lit. "the Chaldean"] king was slain" (Dan. 5:30, AT). The narrator adds that one named "Darius the Mede *received* the kingdom" (v. 31, AT; emphasis added; see ESV, NJPS, NRSV, NKJV, NASB). The New International Version's "took over the kingdom" does not accurately represent the Aramaic verb *qbl*, which means to "receive" or "accept."[23] With this single word, the narrator is telling us that the changing of the top dog in world powers is not due to that top dog's military strength or planning genius. Rather, "the Most High God is sovereign over all kingdoms on earth and sets over them anyone he wishes" (v. 21). It was the living God of the universe who *handed over* the kingdom of Babylon to the Persians. Darius "received" it on behalf of the Medes and Persians. The narrator concludes this story by mentioning Darius's age: sixty-two years (the Aramaic idiom for stating one's age is "a son of sixty-two years") (vv. 30-31 [5:30–6:1 HB]).

Customs and Practices Explained

Great Banquets

In the Old Testament, Daniel 5:1-4 describes a lavish Babylonian royal banquet in the latter half of the sixth century BC (specifically on the night of October 12, 539 BC).[24] At this banquet King Belshazzar hosted one thousand of his kingdom's nobles, plus a group of his wives and concubines. This occurred in the king's palace in the city of Babylon. The narrator highlighted the excessive wine drinking of both the king and his guests at this banquet.

Additionally, the book of Esther mentions several royal banquets given at the Persian royal court in the early fifth century BC (see Esther 1:3, 5, 9; 2:18; 5:5; 7:1). The New International Version gives the name of the

---

23. *Theological Dictionary of the Old Testament: Vol. 16*, 648.
24. Edlin, *Daniel*, 141.

Persian king reigning at that time as Xerxes (Esther 1:1). This is his Greek name. The Hebrew text of Esther, however, gives his name as Ahasuerus (see ESV, NJPS, NRSV, NKJV, NASB); he reigned over the Persian Empire from 486 to 465. Ahasuerus hosted some of these banquets mentioned in Esther; Queen Vashti and Queen Esther hosted others.

King Ahasuerus hosted the first of these royal banquets "in the third year of his reign" (483 BC) in the city of Susa "for a full 180 days" (vv. 3-4). His guests included nobles, officials, military leaders, and princes from throughout the 127 provinces of his kingdom. The purpose was that the king might flaunt "the vast wealth of his kingdom and the splendor and glory of his majesty" (v. 4).

Immediately following that 180-day banquet, King Ahasuerus gave a second, seven-day, palace-garden banquet (v. 5). This was no invitation-only party for only the elite and close friends of the king, however. Rather, all persons found within the city (lit. "citadel") of Susa, from the most important (lit. the "greatest") to those of least account (lit. the "smallest"), were the invited guests (v. 5). The opulence of the setting of this banquet, according to the narrator's description, boggles one's modern-day imagination (v. 6). Whatever else may have been served, the narrator highlighted the wine drinking: "The royal wine was abundant, in keeping with the king's liberality. By the king's command each guest was allowed to drink with no restrictions" (vv. 7-8).

It is from the Greek historians who lived under Persian rule that we learn much outside the Bible of the opulence of the Persian kings' eating habits and royal table needs. Pierre Briant says,

> It is not surprising that royal dinners were not confined to taking nourishment. They made an important social and political statement and had much symbolic value. The king's table, truly a symbol of the king's power . . . , was the preeminent place for gift-giving and royal largesse. In other words, in Persia as elsewhere, the banquet was a festival in every sense of the word, which at the Great King's court was organized according to

the most meticulous rules of protocol. It was a festival organized around the royal person.[25]

God behind the Scenes

Goldingay notes that Daniel 5 portrays an unforeseen overthrow that was not to be taken as a typical military operation or an act of judgment directed at the empire. Instead, it was concentrated on an individual; it depicts the punishment *God* meted out on Belshazzar for his blasphemous behavior. The king's entire person—mentally, physically, and verbally—was implicated in this behavior and in the consequences that ensued.[26]

The Story's Relationship, If Any, to the Other Five Stories or Four Visions in Daniel

Story five (Dan. 5) is related especially to Story four (Dan. 4) in the following two themes:

Human Pride

In story four (Dan. 4), when Daniel confronted King Nebuchadnezzar for his prideful boasting, Nebuchadnezzar repented and humbled himself before the Most High God. God restored his kingdom and extended Nebuchadnezzar's rule. In story five (Dan. 5), when Daniel confronted King Belshazzar for his prideful blasphemy of the Most High God and praise of his own lifeless gods, Belshazzar showed no remorse, no change of heart. God gave no extension of his rule, no second chance. Belshazzar's rule and his life came to an abrupt end.

God's Sovereignty

In story four (Dan. 4), King Nebuchadnezzar recognized that the sovereignty of the Most High God extends over all—over both heaven and earth.

---

25. Pierre Briant, *From Cyrus to Alexander: A History of the Persian Empire*, trans. P. T. Daniels (Winona Lake, IN: Eisenbrauns, 2002), 293.

26. Goldingay, *Daniel*, 287.

In story five (Dan. 5), King Belshazzar did not recognize the sovereignty of the Most High God at all, neither in the heavens nor on the earth.

Faithful Living Today

Each of us needs to continually be mindful, as Daniel reminded King Belshazzar, that God holds in his hand our very "life-breath" (Dan. 5:23, AT). J. Paul Tanner reminds us that at any moment God could take that life-breath from us, if it should be his desire. God lets us live, however, so that our love relationship with him may more and more deepen "and in so doing will serve him from the heart as a gift back to God."[27]

---

27. Tanner, *Daniel*, 359.

11

Story Six (Dan. 6)

Summary

Story six (Dan. 6), as were story four (Dan. 4) and story five (Dan. 5), is an account of royal pride, the pride of Persian king Darius, successor to Babylonian king Belshazzar. In his pride, Darius became an unwitting participant in a conspiracy hatched by certain of his officials, jealous of despised Judean exile Daniel. In so doing, Darius found himself trapped in a scheme from which he was unable to extricate himself, an underhanded scheme in which these wicked conspirators were aiming for Daniel's death.

Their conspiracy backfired, however, when Daniel's God intervened and saved Daniel's life (Dan. 6:22 [v. 23 HB]). The upshot of this whole nefarious affair was that these conspirators themselves, along with their innocent wives and children, were executed by the very method by which they had intended Daniel to be murdered!

The Story

At the very beginning of story six (Dan. 6), the narrator sets the context for the story to follow. Persian king Darius put into place a new structure for governing his large empire, the empire that "he received [*qabbēl*]" (5:31

[6:1 HB], AT) from the Babylonians, a structure that he and succeeding kings would continue to expand. He appointed "120 satraps" to serve as administrators throughout this empire (6:1 [v. 2 HB]). Over these, Darius appointed three administrators, of whom one was Daniel. The purpose of this arrangement, says the narrator, was "so that the king might not suffer loss" (v. 2 [3 HB]). Goldingay observes that "these were government officials generally." They "were the king's viceroys . . . , responsible for security and for the collecting of tribute."[1]

The Term "Satrap"

The English term "satrap(s)" comes to us via the Latin *satrapes*, which is derived from the Greek *satrapēs*. The Greek term is adapted from the Old Persian word *khshathrapāvan*, meaning "protector of the dominion."[2] One can see in the Greek, Latin, and English terms the main *consonants* of the Old Persian term *khshathrapāvan*.

In this way, the narrator alerts us that Daniel, God's counselor to the Babylonian kings in earlier days, is still available. Through him God will make himself known to the Persian royal court.

There was a time lapse between Darius's appointment of Daniel to the high position of administrator (v. 2 [3 HB]) and the narrator's evaluation of Daniel's execution of his duties. In verse 3 (4 HB), the narrator says, "This Daniel *was distinguishing himself* [*mitnaṣṣaḥ*; Dt participle of *nṣḥ* (see the sidebar "The Aramaic Verb *nṣḥ*" on the following page)] among the administrators and the satraps because an excellent spirit was in him" (AT; emphasis added). This latter phrase, observes Jim Edlin, "recalls Nebuchadnezzar's

---

1. Goldingay, *Daniel*, 315.
2. *Merriam-Webster*, s.v. "satrap," accessed November 4, 2022, https://www.merriam-webster.com/dictionary /satrap.

observation that 'the spirit of the holy gods' was in Daniel (4:18). The source of Daniel's excellence was his connection with God."[3]

The Aramaic Verb *nṣḥ*

In Daniel 6:3 (v. 4 HB), "was distinguishing himself" (AT) expresses the participle form of the verb *nṣḥ* in the Dt-stem. It indicates a continual or repetitive action—that is, "time and time again."[4] In Imperial Aramaic, the verb, appearing in official texts, means to "excel." "The servants of the state everywhere were thus admonished to give their best in matters of the king and the empire."[5]

Daniel's execution of his administrative duties was so excellent, excelling above that of the other officials, that King Darius intended to place Daniel administratively "over the whole kingdom" (v. 3 [4 HB]). One is reminded of the Egyptian pharaoh's appointment of Hebrew Joseph to be "in charge of the whole land of Egypt" (Gen. 41:41, 43).

Other administrators and satraps became jealous of Daniel's excellent work. At this point the narrator gives no reason for their jealousy, but later we will hear them remind King Darius of Daniel's lowly status as "one of the *exiles* from Judah" (Dan. 6:13 [v. 14 HB]; emphasis added). In this, we hear an echo of former Babylonian king Belshazzar's sneering royal put-down: "So then, you are Daniel, one of the *exiles* of Judah" (5:13, AT; emphasis added).

Thus, in their jealousy, Daniel's political colleagues "were seeking" (*bā'ayin*; a participle from the verb *b'h* or *b''*, indicating continuous, repetitive action)[6] over a period of time to find some corruption in Daniel (6:4 [v. 5 HB]). Perhaps they were looking for his taking of bribes or his favoring of friends. But, observes the narrator, there was no corruption in him to be

---

3. Edlin, *Daniel*, 153.
4. Tanner, *Daniel*, 371.
5. *Theological Dictionary of the Old Testament: Vol. 16*, 494.
6. L. Koehler, W. Baumgartner, and J. J. Stamm, *Hebrew and Aramaic Lexicon of the Old Testament*, trans. and ed. M. E. J. Richardson, 5 vols. (Leiden, NL: Brill, 1994-99), 1836, Oaktree Software/Accordance.

found. Why? Because, simply put, "he was trustworthy" (*mĕhêman*; a participle from the verb *'mn*, essentially meaning to "be reliable")[7] (v. 4 [5 HB]).

So Daniel's jealous colleagues abandoned their search for a cause to trip up Daniel in the political realm. Rather, they turned to trickery and deceitfulness based on Daniel's loyalty to the God of the universe. Thus they connived together to cook up a trap in which they might catch Daniel in "something to do with the law of his God" (v. 5 [6 HB]). Paul Tanner observes, "It is amazing how the unbelieving world can be so hostile and resentful of God's people gaining influence and authority."[8]

The story will continue to detail a face-off of two irrevocable laws: the law of Daniel's God (v. 5 [6 HB]) and the law of the Medes and Persians (v. 8 [9 HB])—that is, the king's law. The law of the king, when he has made known his ruling, cannot be reversed. But neither can the law of God![9]

The tension in the story, then, is acute. King Darius recognized that Daniel was a "servant of the living God" (v. 20 [21 HB]). But more than that, he was a servant who serves that God "continually" (v. 16 [17 HB]). The Aramaic term that the New International Version translates as "continually" (*bitdîrā'*) carries the nuance of "persistent."[10] Thus Darius is saying that Daniel is a "*persistent* servant of the living God" (AT; emphasis added), not a now-and-then servant, depending on the circumstances. At the same time, the narrator has told us that Daniel is the *trustworthy* and *reliable* servant of King Darius (see comment on v. 4 [5 HB], pp. 118-19).

These conspirators must have thought that certainly no human would be so loyal to a deity, whom no one can see, that that person would risk certain death by disobeying a direct order of his king. So we are left in suspense. As the servant of two kings, which king will Daniel obey: the King of the universe or the king of Persia? Daniel cannot obey both, since, in this case, to obey either requires that he disobey the other!

---

7. *Theological Dictionary of the Old Testament: Vol. 16*, 47.
8. Tanner, *Daniel*, 371.
9. Goldingay, *Daniel*, 318.
10. Koehler, Baumgartner, and Stamm, *Hebrew and Aramaic Lexicon*, 2004.

"So," says the narrator, these jealous officials "brought pressure [*rgš*][11] upon the king" (v. 6 [7 HB], AT), but pressure so subtle that the king was completely unaware of their subterfuge. They claimed to be speaking on behalf of "all" (*kōl*) the king's officials at all levels throughout the king's kingdom (vv. 6-7*a* [7-8*a* HB]). Of this, D. Nolan Fewell says,

> The men are lying, of course, about who has been involved in this agreement. Obviously Daniel has not consented. The story's exposition makes clear, moreover, that . . . the prefects, the counselors and the governors have not been consulted. The lie is a tactic of persuasion. The men lead the king to believe that this opinion poll is exhaustive and unanimous.[12]

Thus, appealing to King Darius's vanity, these conniving officials suggested that he issue a royal edict "in writing so that it cannot be altered— in accordance with the law of the Medes and Persians, which cannot be repealed" (v. 8 [9 HB]). They suggested that the edict should require that for a period of thirty days all persons in Darius's kingdom may pray only to Darius! Anyone caught praying to any other "god or human . . . shall be thrown into the lions' den" (v. 7 [8 HB]). Now, kings in Persia were never regarded as divine.[13] So Darius's caution signals should have been bleeping, alerting him that these officials were devising some nefarious tricks. The narrator gives no clue, but we can only guess that Darius's pride got in the way of his better judgment. Did he not notice that Daniel, his best administrator, was not present among these urging him to issue this decree? It probably did not even occur to him that there might be *anyone* who would disobey the edict of a king, and therefore the threat of the lions' den was rather moot. So why not give it a whirl! He would play god for thirty days! Thus, apparently without further investigation or imagination, Darius "put the [edict] in writing" and, as custom required, surely would have affixed his royal seal to the document (v. 9 [10 HB]).

11. *Theological Dictionary of the Old Testament: Vol. 16*, 703.
12. Danna Nolan Fewell, *Circle of Sovereignty: Plotting Politics in the Book of Daniel*, rev. ed. (Nashville: Abingdon Press, 1991), 109.
13. Goldingay, *Daniel*, 314.

King Darius's conniving officials surely would not have expected Daniel to obey the king's edict. For him to do so would have left them with a lot of explaining to do about why they had come up with this plan in the first place, since, as noted above, Persian kings were never considered divine.

Daniel did not disappoint them. He did not change his daily schedule of prayer to his God! Upon learning of the king's edict, he simply returned to his house and continued ascending daily to his rooftop prayer room. There, from a window opened westward toward the sacred Jerusalem temple (though now in ruins), in full view of all who might pass by, "three times a day he would kneel on his knees and would pray and would give thanks before his God, just as he would do (had been) doing previously" (v. 10 [11 HB], AT).

The four verbs, "would kneel," "would pray," "would give thanks," and "would do," in this sentence are all participles, indicating continuous, repetitive action, descriptive of Daniel's normal life's practice. Since Daniel had been doing this "previously," indicating a longtime practice, his neighbors were no doubt accustomed to seeing this old man on his knees in his upper window. And in a religion-tolerant Persia, anyone observing him might have thought, "Hey, you do your thing and I'll do mine!"

One might imagine that, as Daniel prayed, knowing now that his political associates have turned against him, he might be recalling David's prayer penned long ago amid similar circumstances: "O God, . . . my thoughts trouble me . . . because of what my enemy is saying, because of the threats of the wicked. . . . My heart is in anguish. . . . Fear and trembling have beset me" (Ps. 55:1-5a [vv. 2-6a HB]). Yet David's confidence for deliverance is in God. He affirms, "I [emphatic pronoun], to God I call, and the LORD [yhwh] will save me. Evening and morning and noon I complain and moan, and he hears my voice" (vv. 16-17 [17-18 HB], AT).

Daniel's Age

The time of story six (Dan. 6) is shortly after 539 BC, the year that Babylon fell to the Persians. Daniel was brought to Babylon from Jerusalem in 605 BC. So he has been in Babylon for sixty-six years. He was already at least a teenager when captured. Thus, adding at least fifteen years to his sixty-six years in Babylon, Daniel would be in his early eighties when Darius appointed him to his high administrative post in the empire (v. 2).

The Biblical Postures for Prayer

Both standing and kneeling are noted in the Bible as appropriate postures for prayer. Persons *standing* in prayer are mentioned in 1 Chronicles 23:30; Nehemiah 9:2-3; Matthew 6:5; Mark 11:25; and Luke 18:11, 13. Persons *kneeling* in prayer are mentioned in 1 Kings 8:54; Ezra 9:5; Luke 22:41; Acts 7:60; 9:40; 20:36; and 21:5. Also to be noted is 1 Kings 18:42, where Elijah "bent down [*ghr*] to the ground and put his face between his knees." The verb *ghr*, occurring only three times in the Old Testament, also means to "crouch."[14] Such a position would allow one, by leaning forward, to place his face between his knees.

Expecting to find Daniel ignoring or disobeying King Darius's edict, while observing or obeying his God's law, these conniving officials went as a gang to Daniel's house to confirm what they expected. On observing Daniel in his upper window, in full view, praying to his God, they got their gotcha moment. Rushing to the king, this evil gang of connivers reported, "Daniel, one of those exiles from Judah, doesn't give a thought for you and the legal agreement ['ĕsārā']¹⁵ that you wrote. Rather, three times a day he continues to pray his petition" (v. 13 [14 HB], AT).

At this point, it surely must have dawned on Darius that he had been suckered into a trap. His mind now a whirl, he cast about all day, "until sundown," for how he might rescue his favorite administrator Daniel from being thrown to the lions (v. 14 [15 HB]). Why was "sundown" the cutoff point? Jim Edlin suggests, "This must have been the prescribed period for justice

---

14. *Dictionary of Classical Hebrew*, 2:328.
15. *Theological Dictionary of the Old Testament: Vol. 16*, 70.

to be served on this edict."[16] But all was to no avail. The king's conniving officials wouldn't let him off the hook. Coming to him again, apparently at sundown, they pressed the point that "according to the law of the Medes and Persians" no king-issued decree could be changed (v. 15 [16 HB]). So let's get on with the hanging, so to speak. The king, observes John Goldingay, is in a quandary. If he follows the law, he must allow the unfavorable consequences to unfold. To do otherwise would imperil both the social order and the state.[17]

Time is up. Darius can delay no longer and thus gave the order. Daniel was tossed into the lions' den. By whom? The narrator does not say, but it certainly was not by the conniving officials themselves. Nevertheless, the deed was done. But King Darius spoke a last word to Daniel concerning the possibility of "rescue." If rescue is possible, it is now in the realm of "your God, whom you consistently and insistently [see discussion of the term *bit-dîrā'* above among comments on v. 5, p. 119] serve" (v. 16 [17 HB], AT). The meaning of the verb form that Darius used, *yĕšêzĕbinnāk*, is ambiguous: it can be translated as "May he rescue you!" "Can he rescue you?" "Will he rescue you?" or "He must rescue you!" Goldingay opts for "He must deliver you," adding that it is unclear, however, whether Darius is challenging God, making an affirmation of faith, or expressing a melancholy hope.[18] Perhaps, however, we hear Darius saying, "Daniel, it is out of my hands. Even as king of the most powerful kingdom on earth, I can do nothing to rescue you. If you are to be rescued, a power greater than I must act" (v. 16 [17 HB], author's paraphrase).

There is a certain irony in the narrator's comment concerning the king's and nobles' signet rings: not only was the stone that covered the den's opening "sealed" with them, but as Goldingay observes, so was the seeming end

---

16. Edlin, *Daniel*, 157.
17. Goldingay, *Daniel*, 321.
18. Ibid., 304, 321.

of Daniel sealed.[19] The seals were impressed into either wax[20] or soft clay.[21] They would not be broken until the next morning (v. 17 [18 HB]).

We are told nothing of how those conniving officials spent that night. Maybe they held a party, celebrating Daniel's presumed death. Or maybe they slept deeply, believing they had gotten rid of this religious fanatic. We can only imagine. The narrator, however, does tell us of Darius's restless, miserable night: he declined food and entertainment; even sleep eluded him (v. 18 [19 HB]).

The next morning, not even waiting for the full light of day, "at the first light of dawn," Darius rushed to the lions' den (v. 19 [20 HB]). Perhaps he broke the seals himself. Certainly others would have removed the heavy stone covering the den's mouth on his behalf. His voice choking with emotion, he called down into the den, "Daniel, servant of the living God, has your God, whom you insistently/consistently serve, has he been able to rescue you from the lions?" (v. 20 [21 HB], AT).

The Living God

In Daniel 6:20 (v. 21 HB), King Darius calls out to Daniel in the lions' den, "Daniel, servant of the living God, has your God . . . been able to rescue you from the lions?" John Goldingay insightfully comments that by referring to the "living God" in the question about Daniel's possible deliverance, the king lightly touches on the correct response to his inquiry. That is, as the Old Testament affirms, God is not only living but also all-powerful and fully capable of both judging and blessing.[22]

The title "living God" occurs in the mouths of others elsewhere in the Old Testament:

- Moses: "the voice of the living God speaking out of fire" at Mount Sinai (Deut. 5:26).

---

19. Ibid., 321.
20. Tanner, *Daniel*, 385.
21. Edlin, *Daniel*, 158.
22. Goldingay, *Daniel*, 322.

- Joshua: "You will know that the living God is among you" (Josh. 3:10).
- David: "Who is this uncircumcised Philistine that he should defy the armies of the living God?" (1 Sam. 17:26).
- Hezekiah: "the field commander, whom his master, the king of Assyria, has sent to ridicule the living God" (2 Kings 19:4; cf. Isa. 37:4).
- Jeremiah: "But the LORD [yhwh] is the true God; he is the living God, the eternal King" (Jer. 10:10).
- Hosea: "Yet the Israelites . . . will be called 'children of the living God'" (Hos. 1:10 [2:1 HB]).
- Sons of Korah: "My soul thirsts for God, for the living God" (Ps. 42:2 [3 HB]).

Responding with full respect for Darius—"May the king live forever"—Daniel assured him that he was alive and well (v. 21 [22 HB]). "My God sent his angel, and he shut the mouths of the lions" (v. 22 [23 HB]). There is a play on "mouth" here: just as the stone was "placed over the mouth [pum] of the den" of lions and thus shut Daniel in (v. 17 [18 HB]), so God's angel "shut the mouths [pum] of the lions" to protect Daniel (v. 22 [23 HB]). Daniel credited his rescue by God's angel to his having been judged in the heavenly court, so to speak, and "found innocent in [God's] eyes" and also not guilty of any harm (in his political duties) before the king (v. 22 [23 HB], AT).

King Darius "was exceedingly pleased at this" (v. 23 [24 HB], AT) and ordered that Daniel be brought up from the den. How was this done? Certainly (in light of v. 24 [25 HB]) no one dared go down in there to lift him out; so the lifters must have lowered ropes to Daniel to wrap around himself. However it was done, when Daniel was lifted out into the light of the morning and checked over—and here the narrator structured his sentence so that it reads—"no harm was found on him who trusted in his God" (v. 23 [24 HB], AT). The New International Version's insertion of the word "because" is not in the Aramaic, nor is it implied. The narrator is making a statement about the lifelong relationship of this man Daniel with "his God."

The story concludes with King Darius issuing *two commands*, one tragic, the other God honoring. Now fully wise to the conniving plot of those political administrators who had trapped him into this nefarious plan to murder Daniel, Darius's *first command* was that they, their wives, and their children be tossed into the lions' den. These lions must have been ravenous, for the narrator paints a gruesome picture of the connivers' bodies not even reaching the floor before "the lions overpowered them and crushed all their bones" (v. 24 [25 HB]).

Darius's *second command* was much broader. It was "a decree" issued "to all the nations and peoples of every language in all the earth" or, to put it more realistically, "in every part of my kingdom" (vv. 25-26 [26-27 HB]). The title or heading of this decree may have been "The God of Daniel." This was followed with an urging of the people's *duty* to "fear and reverence" this God (v. 26 [27 HB]). Then the king appended a list of *reasons why*: "he is the living God," "he endures forever," "his kingdom will not be destroyed," "his dominion will never end," "he rescues and he saves," and "he performs signs and wonders" both "in the heavens and on the earth" (vv. 26-27 [27-28 HB]). The king then capped it all off with a *why* he is issuing this edict: Because "he [Daniel's God] has rescued Daniel from the power of the lions" (v. 27 [28 HB]).

The narrator added a final brief historical note in which there is an Aramaic *waw* conjunction that may be translated as either "and" or "that is." Virtually all English versions opt for "and," taking the conjunction as a conjunctive, connecting Daniel's success in his special administrative position throughout the reign of Darius and on into the reign of Cyrus. Yet this conjunction may also be taken as an explicative and translated "that is." The sentence would then read, "So Daniel was successful throughout the reign of Darius, that is [*waw*], the reign of Cyrus the Persian" (v. 28 [29 HB], AT). Thus the narrator is explaining that Darius and Cyrus are the same person.

Customs and Practices Explained

The Persian System of Satrapies

In story six (Dan. 6) the narrator mentions that Darius the Mede (see 5:31 for this title, p. 112), who may actually be King Cyrus (see 6:28 [v. 29 HB], p. 126, and the sidebar "Who Was Darius the Mede?" in section titled "The Sixth Story [Dan. 6]," in ch. 4, "Chapter Summaries," p. 32), in 539 BC appointed "120 satraps to rule throughout the kingdom" (v. 1 [2 HB]). He does not, however, equate these satraps with ruling over 120 satrapies or provinces in the kingdom. Only later, under the reign of Darius I (r. 522–485 BC), or so it seems, the empire was divided into twenty satrapies. It is the fifth-century BC Greek historian Herodotus who includes this bit of information (along with a description of how Darius I funded his operations) in his extensive history of the Greco-Persian wars:

> [Darius] divided his dominions into twenty governments, called by the Persians satrapies; and doing so and appointing governors, he ordained that each several nation should pay him tribute. . . . Therefore it is seen by adding all together that Darius collected a yearly tribute of fourteen thousand five hundred and sixty talents. . . . The tribute is stored by the king in this fashion: he melts it down and pours it into earthen vessels; when the vessel is full he breaks the earthenware away, and when he needs money cuts off as much as will serve his purpose.[23]

The Law of the Medes and Persians

In story six (Dan. 6), Daniel's adversaries appeal three times to the unchangeableness of what they call "the law of the Medes and Persians" (Dan. 6:8, 12, 15 [vv. 9, 13, 16 HB], AT) as the reason why Darius the Mede, in 539 BC, could not or dare not revoke, or allow an exception to, an edict that he had issued. This edict stated that for the succeeding thirty days, no

---

23. A. D. Godley, trans., *Herodotus*, vol. 2 of 4 vols. (1921; repr., London: Heinemann, 1928), 117-25, Internet Archive, https://archive.org/details/herodotuswitheng02herouoft/page/n7/mode/2up.

person in his kingdom, on the penalty of death, was to pray to any human or deity except to himself (v. 7 [8 HB]).

Later, in the third year (Esther 1:3) of the reign of Persian king Xerxes (Ahasuerus) (r. 486-465 BC), Memukan, one of Xerxes's wise men or nobles, advised the king to "issue a royal decree and let it be written in the laws of Persia and Media, which cannot be repealed" (v. 19) that Queen Vashti was never again to be allowed to appear before the king. As the story of King Xerxes and his new (Jewish) queen, Esther, unfolds, Xerxes has Mordecai the Jew compose a decree "in the king's name" granting the Jews throughout the Persian Empire "the right to assemble and protect themselves" (v. 11) against their enemies in their soon-to-occur attempt to exterminate them as a people. Though the king does not use the phrase "law [or laws] of the Medes and Persians," he does note that "no document written in the king's name and sealed with his ring can be revoked" (v. 8).

Outside the biblical references cited, there is little support in the historical sources for the unchangeableness of Median and Persian law.

Jews Praying toward Jerusalem

Daniel 6:10 notes that Daniel faced toward Jerusalem when he prayed three times daily on his rooftop. There is no command in the Old Testament that Jews were to face toward the land of Judah, the city of Jerusalem, or the temple when they prayed. Many Old Testament students, however, point to Solomon's prayer at the dedication of the Jerusalem temple (1 Kings 8) as a possible context that gave rise to the practice after the destruction of the temple in 587 BC at the hands of the Babylonian army.[24] The portion of Solomon's prayer referenced is verses 35-36: "When the heavens are shut up and there is no rain because your people have sinned against you, and when they pray *toward this place* and give praise to your name and turn from their sin because you have afflicted them, then hear from heaven and forgive the sin of your servants, your people Israel" (emphasis added). Tanner speculates,

---

24. See, for example, Edlin, *Daniel*, 156; Goldingay, *Daniel*, 316; Tanner, *Daniel*, 382.

In his prayer, Solomon looked ahead to the days when the Jewish people would be taken away into exile because of their sins. . . . Yet, if while they were in exile they would humble themselves, repent, and pray toward the place where their temple had once stood, God would forgive them and restore them from captivity. . . . Daniel was being faithful to do this.[25]

Punishment of Offenders and Their Families Equal to the Offense

In Daniel 6:24, when King Darius tossed Daniel's accusers to the lions, he is invoking what has come to be called the "law of retaliation" (Lat., *lex talionis*), first encoded in the early Babylonian Code of Hammurabi. This law is often referred to as "an eye for an eye." It provided that a person who has caused injury to another or by false witness has intended to cause injury to another is to receive punishment equal to the injury caused or intended. That these conniving officials should be put to death in Daniel's place, then, is in keeping with both ancient Mesopotamian practice and Old Testament law (see Deut. 19:16-21; Esther 7:9-10; Prov. 19:5, 9; 21:28). We also note instances in the Old Testament of family members suffering punishment along with the offender (see Num. 16:27-33; Josh. 7:14-25; Esther 9:25; Isa. 13:15-16).

God behind the Scenes

God's Angel

One must assume that God was already planning his rescue operation of Daniel even before Daniel's accusers set *their* plan in motion that would lead to his death. They surely did not expect Daniel to survive a toss into a den of lions. After all, who was this invisible God he prayed to every day? Surely he was a nobody.

---

25. Tanner, *Daniel*, 382.

As Daniel was led to the lions' den, he spoke not a word, seeming to go calmly to whatever his fate would be. One wonders, though, if he might have been recalling the similar experience of his three Jewish conscript friends, Shadrach, Meshach, and Abednego, when tossed into the "blazing furnace" many years earlier (Dan. 3:23). *Their* God, who was also *his* God, had "sent his angel and rescued his servants!" so King Nebuchadnezzar had testified (v. 28). Would God send his angel again to rescue *him*? Daniel might have been wondering. Perhaps he recalled the affirmation of the anonymous psalmist of Psalm 91: "Whoever dwells in the shelter of the Most High will rest in the shadow of the Almighty. . . . If you say, 'The LORD is my refuge,' and you make the Most High your dwelling, . . . he will command his angels concerning you to guard you in all your ways" (vv. 1, 9, 11). Or maybe the words of David in Psalm 34 came to him: "The angel of the LORD encamps around those who fear him, and he delivers them" (v. 7 [8 HB]).

Indeed, the next morning, upon being taken from the lions' den unscathed, Daniel gave witness: "My God sent his angel, and he shut the mouths of the lions" (Dan. 6:22 [v. 23 HB]). Jim Edlin observes that "the angel was sent from God. The primary explanation for his preservation is the saving initiative of God."[26]

The Story's Relationship, If Any, to the Other Five Stories or Four Visions in Daniel

Story six (Dan. 6) is parallel to story three (Dan. 3), since both stories involve discord and scheming at the royal court and the downfall and restoration of a high-level state official.[27] In each story, at the instigation of jealous court officials, a pagan king in the Babylonian court issued an edict that placed impossible religious requirements upon certain Judean exiles in positions of political authority.

---

26. Edlin, *Daniel*, 159.
27. Goldingay, *Daniel*, 307.

In story 3 (Dan. 3) Babylonian king Nebuchadnezzar's edict was phrased in such a way that it demanded that Judean exiles Shadrach, Meshach, and Abednego—"Jews whom [the king had] set over the affairs of the province of Babylon" (3:12)—betray their sole allegiance to the God of Israel and publicly worship the king's huge image of gold (vv. 5, 7). In story six (Dan. 6) Persian king Darius the Mede's edict was also phrased in such a way that it, too, demanded that Judean exile Daniel—whom the king had appointed as one of three administrators over the Persian kingdom (6:2)—should abandon prayer to the God of Israel and pray only to King Darius (vv. 6-9).

In both cases, these Judean exiles, facing arrest and surely death, remained steadfastly loyal to the God of Israel. In both cases, God sent a heavenly rescuer, "and others die in their place."[28]

Faithful Living Today

Perhaps some readers of story 6 (Dan. 6) may interpret God's miraculous rescue of Daniel from death in the lions' den as a guarantee that God will always deliver his faithful ones from similar circumstances. Surely there have been many who have experienced miraculous deliverances similar to that of Daniel. We can read Luke's witness of early Christians' deliverances in Acts 5:19-20; 12:1-10; and 16:19-26. We may read the published testimonials of faithful believers of all nationalities and languages down through the past two thousand years whose lives have been spared in spite of orders by cruel dictators, despots, and captors that their lives be taken. At the same time, we are told of and read of the many, numbering into the thousands, even into the millions, whose lives have been snuffed out because of their faithful adherence to God's law rather than humankind's.

Goldingay astutely observes that Daniel 6 is not saying that faithful witnesses can look forward to a martyrdom-free life, although God does sometimes deliver his people from death and from other perils—such as injustice

---

28. Ibid., 312.

and fear. In this life, some will find deliverance from death, and others will not. Yet the message of Daniel—especially Daniel 12:1-3—is not just to set our sights before death but also beyond it for our deliverance. It is then the resurrection of Christ that is the firm basis for our hope.[29]

---

29. Ibid., 323-24.

12

Vision One (Dan. 7)

Summary

In vision one (Dan. 7) we read about Daniel's first dream vision, occurring in 550 or 549 BC, Belshazzar's first year of rule in Babylon (7:1).[1] The vision takes us "to the end of history."[2] In this vision Daniel saw four beasts rising from a sea; out of the fourth came a little horn "speaking great things" (v. 8, AT) "against the Most High" (v. 25).

Daniel also saw a court judgment scene in which the "Ancient of Days" and others sat upon thrones while "books were opened" (vv. 9-10). There, a figure described as "one like a son of man" joined them (v. 13). Judgment was passed upon the four beasts and little horn, stripping them of all earthly authority. This authority was handed over to the "one like a son of man" (v. 14) and to "the holy people of the Most High" (v. 27).

---

1. Gerhard F. Hasel, "The First and Third Years of Belshazzar (Daniel 7:1; 8:1)," *Andrews University Seminary Studies* 15, no. 2 (1977): 162, 168.
2. Longman, *How to Read Daniel*, 97.

The Vision

It was to be a strange night for Daniel. The narrator gives nothing of the context or circumstances other than that Daniel had apparently retired for the night—he was "upon his bed" (Dan. 7:1, AT). Sometime after falling asleep, Daniel dreamed (lit. "saw a dream"), not an ordinary, every-night kind of dream, though. In this one, unusual scene after scene passed through his sleeping mind. "Visions" both the narrator and Daniel called them (vv. 1-2). In the Old Testament, visions speak of an audiovisual experience, sometimes while sleeping, sometimes while awake, in which one in some way encounters God's presence. Daniel didn't understand the meaning of that night's dream visions. Yet their potential significance so grabbed him that he wasted no time in writing up a summary of them (v. 1).

Daniel's Vision (Dan. 7:2-28)

Daniel tells of his vision in the first person. He presents it in *three scenes*: the *first scene* takes place in or from a *sea* (vv. 2-8), the *second scene* takes place on or around a *throne* (vv. 9-14), and the *third scene* gives the interpretation of the first two (vv. 15-28).

Scene One: The Great Sea (Dan. 7:2-8)

Daniel first observed a great storm of hurricane force, driven by the "four winds of heaven" (v. 2). The mention of "four suggests totality"[3] and implies that the wind is coming from all four geographical points at once—east, west, north, and south. These winds are causing the "great sea" to rage (v. 2; this possibly should be capitalized as "Great Sea," elsewhere in the Old Testament the title of what we call the Mediterranean Sea [cf. ESV and NIV of Josh. 1:4]).[4] Emerging from this raging sea, Daniel observed four large animals; each one was unique (v. 3).

The first large animal has combined characteristics of *a lion and an eagle* (v. 4). The lion of Old Testament times is known for its ferociousness,

---

3. Goldingay, *Daniel*, 386.
4. *Theological Dictionary of the Old Testament: Vol. 16*, 352.

strength, and courage. The eagle is swift in flight, a raptor—that is, a bird of prey. But what the New International Version here translates as an "eagle" (nĕšar in both Aramaic and Hebrew), the zoologists believe to be the griffon vulture (see also Hab. 1:8: nešer ["vultures," ISV]), a carrion eater. With a wingspan of some nine feet, it is the largest bird of Israel, though now nearly extinct.[5] Even as Daniel watched, this animal's wings were plucked off, it was made to stand upright on two feet as a man, and it was given a human's mind (lit. "heart") (Dan. 7:4).

The second large animal appeared right after the first, perhaps almost simultaneously. It resembled *a bear*, an animal that also causes great fear in humans. This bear is depicted in an odd position: raised up on one side (v. 5). What does Daniel mean? Perhaps it is rearing up on its hind legs, standing in a humanlike position, indicating that it, too, has some humanlike qualities. Or maybe it is simply deformed, showing "a disproportioned growth on one of its sides."[6] Additionally, it is said to have "three ribs in its mouth between its teeth" (v. 5). What is meant by this? Are the ribs a deformity? Edlin suggests the vision may intend them to be understood as "tusks" or "fangs."[7] Since an offstage voice (whose? God's?) has told this animal "Stand up, eat much flesh" (v. 5, AT), this would make doing so easier.

The third large animal to emerge from the sea as Daniel continued to look resembled *a leopard* (v. 6). Though not as large as a lion or a bear, leopards instill great fear in humans. The leopard is known in the Old Testament for its spots (Jer. 13:23) and its swiftness (Hab. 1:8). In Daniel's vision, this animal, too, was not a normal looking leopard. Four bird wings sprouted from its back, and it had four heads—one assumes these were attached to a neck where normally one head would have been! Why four wings and four heads? Perhaps, as with the four winds of heaven (Dan. 7:2), four indicates "totality or universal activity" or simply the multiplicity indicates a capacity

---

5. Ibid., 510; Azaria Alon, *The Natural History of the Land of the Bible* (Garden City, NY: Doubleday, 1978), 220-21.

6. Edlin, *Daniel*, 174.

7. Ibid.

for swift multidirectional movement.[8] This creature is somewhat analogous to the four living creatures in Ezekiel's vision by the Kebar River in Babylonia: each had four faces and four wings (Ezek. 1:1-6). Daniel adds a nonphysical aspect to his comments about the leopard. Someone gave the beast "authority to rule" (Dan. 7:6). But who? He does not say.

The fourth large animal to emerge from the sea in Daniel's night vision is unidentified as to kind. He simply notes that it was terrifying, frightening, and exceedingly powerful (v. 7). Moreover, its teeth were large and made of iron. Daniel uses the Semitic dual form (two of) for teeth but apparently is not referring to two *teeth* but to its two *jaws* of teeth.[9] Then, very descriptively, Daniel says of this animal, "[It was] devouring and crushing and trampling with its feet the remainder [the leftovers?]" (v. 7, AT). Indeed, it was unlike the previous three large animals. It was "different," says Daniel, because "it had ten horns" (v. 7). Where? One supposes they protruded from its head.

Daniel continues: "I was contemplating about the [ten] horns. And, behold, another horn, a little one, emerged among them" (v. 8, AT). He observed that as this little horn emerged, three of the original ten "horns were uprooted before it" (v. 8). The Aramaic passive "were uprooted" suggests that possibly the little horn does not do the uprooting but rather that this is God's doing as though God were making room for the little horn (v. 8*a*).[10]

A unique aspect of this new little horn was that it had eyes—eyes like human eyes! And it had a mouth—and this "mouth was speaking great things" (v. 8*b*, AT). The New International version's "spoke boastfully" is interpretive on the part of the translators, for the text here is neither negative nor positive. (Only later does the vision interpreter [see v. 16] indicate that

---

8. Goldingay, *Daniel*, 359.
9. Ibid., 335, n. 4.b.
10. Ibid., 360.

this fourth animal "will speak against the Most High," which may be interpreted as boastful speaking [see v. 25].)

Scene Two: The Throne Room (Dan. 7:9-14)

As Daniel continued looking, the sea is no longer in focus; rather, the scene of his vision changed to that of a throne room, alias a courtroom. Where is it located? Paul Tanner understands the throne room to be in heaven; John Goldingay, on earth; and John Collins suggests the whole vision takes place "simply in mythic space."[11] Unspecified attendants set thrones in place in preparation for an impending judgment. Among these thrones is a special or central one upon which one called "the Ancient of Days sat down" (v. 9a, AT). Why the plural "thrones"? The plural cannot be dismissed as simply suggesting an oversize throne for the main throne or a portion of the furnishings, as Goldingay suggests.[12] Yet the identity of those who occupy the thrones other than the main throne cannot be determined; the best we can say is that the text intends that we understand them to be part of the "court [that or who] sat" in verse 10 (AT). They were to give counsel and advice to the one called "the Ancient of Days" in their midst. Paul Tanner observes, "The main thing is the Ancient of Days is the one pronouncing and enacting judgment; others are there to witness the event and glorify God who righteously judges."[13]

The designation "Ancient of Days" (*'atîq yômîn*) does not necessarily refer to one who is "old" as in human terms of one who is "aged." In Imperial Aramaic, *'atîq* "consistently refers to objects from earlier times that do not age as people do. Thus, the 'Ancient of Days' on his divine throne . . . denotes an age beyond the typical human lifespan. . . . [Therefore,] 'an Ancient of Days' . . . does not mean an old person, but a transcendent figure . . . that has

11. Tanner, *Daniel*, 421; Goldingay, *Daniel*, 361; John J. Collins, *Daniel: A Commentary on the Book of Daniel*, Hermeneia (Minneapolis: Fortress Press, 1993), 303, Internet Archive, https://archive.org/details/danielcommentary0000coll/page/n5/mode/2up.

12. Goldingay, *Daniel*, 361.

13. Tanner, *Daniel*, 423.

existed since primeval times."[14] Though neither Daniel nor his interpreter says this person seated on the throne is God, the vision appears to assume this to be so (v. 9a).

Daniel's description of the Ancient of Days focuses on his clothing, which he says is "white as snow" and on his hair which is "pure as wool" (v. 9b, AT). These may be "features associated with someone respected and wise" but also alluding to "God's holiness."[15]

What Daniel notes especially about the throne of the Ancient of Days is fire. It is enveloped with fire! His descriptions are cryptic: "his throne, flames of fire"; "its wheels, burning fire" (v. 9c, AT; cf. the fire and wheels of God's chariot in Ezekiel's vision [Ezek. 1:13-15]); and "a river of fire flowing, emerging from before him" (Dan. 7:10a, AT). This is consistent with other scenes in the Old Testament where fire is associated with God in a number of ways, one of which is a symbol of judgment[16] (see Deut. 4:24; Pss. 18:8-13 [vv. 9-14 HB]; 21:9 [v. 10 HB]; 50:3; 97:3; Isa. 66:15-16; Ezek. 21:31-32 [vv. 36-37 HB]; Amos 5:6).

In this scene in Daniel 7, surrounding the Ancient of Days, besides those who sit upon the many thrones, is his numberless otherworldly army of created beings, normally unseen by humans. The best Daniel can say is that attending him were "thousands upon thousands . . . ten thousand times ten thousand" (v. 10b). We catch a few glimpses of these attendants elsewhere in the Old Testament—for example, "myriads of holy ones" (Deut. 33:2), "the multitudes of heaven" (1 Kings 22:19), and "the chariots of God are tens of thousands and thousands of thousands" (Ps. 68:17 [v. 18 HB]).

In Job 38:4, 7, in God's challenge to Job, we have a privileged glimpse of God's otherworldly beings whom he had created even before he had created any human being, in fact, even before he had created the world: "Where were you when I laid the earth's foundation? . . . while the morning stars sang

---

14. *Theological Dictionary of the Old Testament: Vol. 16*, 601.
15. Edlin, *Daniel*, 176.
16. Ibid.; Goldingay, *Daniel*, 362.

together and all the angels shouted for joy?" Of this otherworldly glimpse, John Hartley comments, "On the occasion of laying the earth's cornerstone, *the morning stars* were assembled as an angelic chorus to sing praises to God for the glory of his world. At the moment the stone was set in place *the sons of God*, i.e., the angels, broke out in joyous singing, praising God, the Creator."[17]

Daniel notes that the throne-room setup of Daniel 7, in fact, doubles as a courtroom where a judgment is about to take place. Thus we read, "The court sat and the books were opened" (v. 10c, AT). What are "the books"?

Edlin notes that "the tradition of God keeping records of human behavior within his realm runs deep in the Hebrew Scriptures (Exod 32:32; Ps 56:8; Mal 3:16)."[18] Goldingay observes that reviewing books for past actions and events was a practice of the king's court.[19] (See subsection titled "Royal Record Keeping ['The Books Were Opened' (Dan. 7:10c)]," in section titled "Customs and Practices Explained," p. 147.)

Could these "books" of Daniel 7 be, as Tanner suggests, an Old Testament reference to "the record of the works and ungodly acts of unbelievers, which they will be confronted with at the great white throne judgment [see Rev. 20:12-15]? . . . The records in these books in Daniel present *the evidence* that they [the unbelievers] do not measure up to the righteousness of."[20]

The court of the Ancient of Days wasted no time! As Daniel watched, it found the fourth beast guilty of insolence: its little horn was speaking "great [NIV: "boastful"] words or things," apparently against the Ancient of Days (Dan. 7:11, AT). Jim Edlin observes that "God does not tolerate insolence within his domain."[21] Sentence on the fourth beast was swift: it was killed, and its body utterly destroyed by fire (v. 11). (See subsection titled

---

17. John E. Hartley, *The Book of Job*, New International Commentary on the Old Testament (Grand Rapids: Eerdmans, 1988), 495 (italics original).
18. Edlin, *Daniel*, 176.
19. Goldingay, *Daniel*, 362.
20. Tanner, *Daniel*, 424 (italics original).
21. Edlin, *Daniel*, 177.

"Punishment by Burning [Dan. 7:11]," in section titled "Customs and Practices Explained," p. 147.)

While Daniel continued to watch, this court also judged the first three beasts, but their sentence was less harsh than that of the fourth beast. The court allowed them to go on living "for a period of time," but at some point each would lose its "power" or "dominion" (*šālṭān*; v. 12, AT). Daniel's interpreter (within his vision) will give him the meaning of these four beasts in the scheme of world history later in his dream (see comments on vv. 17-27, pp. 142-45).

Verses 13-14 describe the climax of Daniel's night dream vision, the most significant scene of all, toward which the vision has been moving. The Aramaic *order* of Daniel's first two phrases (which the NIV does not maintain) is significant: "Behold, with or among the clouds of the heavens, one like a son of man was coming" (AT). Goldingay comments that the phrase about "the clouds of the heavens" directs us to heaven and to the one approaching the court.[22] Edlin notes that elsewhere in the Old Testament, "God rides the clouds like a king in a chariot (Pss. 18:9-12; 68:4; 104:3; Isa. 19:1)."[23] This figure "like a son of man" arrived from heaven to the earthly visionary throne room and was ushered into the presence of the Ancient of Days, by whom Daniel does not say (Dan. 7:13).

In stark contrast, what was taken from the first three beasts of the previous scene—"dominion" [*šālṭān*] (v. 12, AT [NIV: "authority"])—in this scene, the court of the Ancient of Days awarded to the figure who was "like a son of man" (i.e., "dominion" [*šālṭān*]; v. 14, AT). In addition, he was given "glory and sovereign power" and "an everlasting dominion that will not pass away" (v. 14). Moreover, Daniel saw peoples of every nation and language turn to this figure and worship him (v. 14).

So, who is this "son of man" figure? Scholars, both Jewish and Christian, have proposed several possible identifications over the centuries. Since

---

22. Goldingay, *Daniel*, 364.
23. Edlin, *Daniel*, 178.

Daniel 7 does not offer any clues, "readers are left to interpret this person in light of other scriptures."[24] For Christians, the best interpretation for Daniel's visionary "one like a son of man" is messianic, fulfilled in Jesus Christ the Messiah.[25] Jesus used the title "son of man" for himself multiple times in the four gospels. In four of these he seems to clearly associate the title with Daniel 7. He speaks of "sitting at the right hand of the Mighty One and coming on the clouds of heaven" (Mark 14:62; Matt. 26:64; cf. 24:30), that "he will sit on his glorious throne," and that "all the nations will be gathered before him" (Matt. 25:31-32). Edlin also points to Paul's description of Jesus in Philippians 2:6-11 with features of the "son of man" figure in Daniel 7:[26] "Christ Jesus: Who, being in very nature God, . . . made in human likeness. . . . at the name of Jesus every knee should bow . . . and every tongue acknowledge that Jesus Christ is Lord" (Phil. 2:5-7, 10-11).

Scene Three: The Interpretation (Dan. 7:15-27)

At this point Daniel expressed his emotional response to these dream visions that he was seeing in his head: "My spirit was troubled, . . . my mind [lit. "my head"] alarmed me" (v. 15, AT).

We now learn that there were others standing nearby within the vision. They were apparently angelic or heavenly beings and were also watching what was happening in the throne room (courtroom). So approaching one of them, Daniel asked him if he could give him "the meaning of all this" (v. 16; lit. "reliable [knowledge] concerning all this").[27] This angelic being did not hesitate; he "made known to me," said Daniel, "the interpretation of the things" that he had seen in his vision (v. 16, AT).

The Aramaic text here does not identify this angelic being who became Daniel's vision interpreter, but perhaps we are given a clue later in 9:21. There, while in prayer, says Daniel, "Gabriel, the man I had seen in the

---

24. Ibid., 179.
25. Ibid.; Tanner, *Daniel*, 440.
26. Edlin, *Daniel*, 179.
27. *Theological Dictionary of the Old Testament: Vol. 16*, 359.

earlier vision, came to me." To what "earlier vision" is Daniel referring? It *may* be the vision he experienced here in vision one (Dan. 7). If he is, the archangel Gabriel is a viable candidate as Daniel's interpreter of his vision here in 7:16.

The angelic interpreter gave Daniel a very brief initial overview of what the four beasts signify: they "are four kings that will rise from the earth" (v. 17). Since a kingdom is represented by its king, then the reverse is also true.[28] Since the angelic interpreter in no way even hints at the identity of these kings-kingdoms, scholars have proposed several sequences of specific historical kings or empires and sometimes have fiercely defended their positions. The main proposals are these: (1) the four Babylonian kings who reigned within Daniel's lifetime—that is, Nebuchadnezzar, Amel-Marduk, Neriglissar, and Nabonidus, and (2) the four kingdoms or empires known as (*a*) Babylon, Media, Persia, and Greece or (*b*) Babylon, Persia, Greece, and Rome.[29] Though a case can be made for each scheme, none are without difficulties.

Jim Edlin's Interpretation of the Four Beasts

Regarding Daniel 7:17, Jim Edlin suggests that (1) the vision's four beasts are representative of all human history; (2) the four kings-kingdoms are representative of all this world's kingdoms together; (3) the first beast or first kingdom-king represents Babylon and/or its first king, Nebuchadnezzar; (4) the fourth beast or fourth kingdom represents history's final political power, whenever that may be; and (5) the second and third beasts or kingdoms, of which the interpreter says nothing, could signify other political powers occurring in history between the first and last kingdoms.[30]

Daniel's angelic interpreter now speaks of "the holy people of the Most High"; he says that they "will receive the kingdom and will possess it

---

28. Goldingay, *Daniel*, 371.
29. Edlin, *Daniel*, 181-82.
30. Ibid., 181.

forever—yes, for ever and ever" (v. 18). Who are these "holy people"? As suggested earlier, "one like a son of man," for Christians, is Jesus Christ the Messiah. Tanner draws attention to verse 14, in which "the Lord Jesus . . . is given the kingdom in which all will serve and obey him. As with any kingdom, . . . he has subjects."[31] This, Tanner finds, sheds light on the identity of the "holy people" of verse 18; "the subjects [in Jesus's kingdom] are the 'holy ones of the Most High,' i.e., the people of God who are rightly related to him."[32]

Daniel was not satisfied with the angelic interpreter's summary interpretation of his vision, given in verses 17-18. So Daniel pressed him to reveal more, especially concerning the fourth beast and the (smaller) horn on its head that, upon emerging, had pushed aside three other horns.

Daniel described this fourth beast as "exceedingly terrifying" (v. 19, AT), for he now noticed what he had not seen earlier—it not only had "teeth or iron" but "claws of bronze," presumably on all four feet; "it was eating and crushing, and trampling with his feet what remained" (v. 19, AT). It was the *claws*, suggests Tanner, that magnified the destructive character of the kingdom that this beast represented.[33]

But what about the horn that displaced three others on the fourth beast's head? As Daniel watched, this horn was warring against God's "holy people," and it appeared to be winning! (v. 21). How could this be? But, then, as Daniel continued watching, the Ancient of Days, the one from the earlier throne-room scene (v. 9)—God, the divine Judge—appeared on the scene. He "pronounced the judgment" between the warring parties, "in favor of the saints of the Most High" (v. 22, AT). This turned the battle against the fourth beast, so that God's saints "possessed the kingdom" (v. 22).

The angelic interpreter again explained that the fourth beast symbolized a fourth kingdom, different from all other earthly kingdoms. Its devouring,

---

31. Tanner, *Daniel*, 448.
32. Ibid.
33. Ibid., 453.

trampling, and crushing will affect a large swath of humanity, symbolized by the hyperbole the "whole earth" (v. 23).

The ten horns, the interpreter explained, symbolized ten kings coming from this fourth kingdom. Scholars have suggested and contrived various schemes of ten kingdoms or nations in past history, or even yet to come, for the fulfilment of these ten. Yet there is no agreement. Ten in the Bible symbolizes fulfillment or completeness, and it may well carry that meaning here, rather than a set number. That is, when people think the time for history's succession of kingdoms is nearing its completion, still another powerful king or ruler, the small horn, will arise, overpowering three kings (v. 24). What does "three" symbolize? Edlin draws attention to Ecclesiastes 4:12: "A cord of three strands is not quickly broken." Thus, says Edlin, "three things create a strong bond"; three kings, he suggests, "is more likely symbolic of extra strength" (Dan. 7:24).[34]

This last king in Daniel's vision, says the angelic interpreter, will, *first*, "speak against the Most High" (v. 25). Though this horn-king has eyes and a mouth and speaks like a human being (vv. 8, 20), in speaking against God, it will aspire to the supernatural and will challenge heaven itself. This is like the king in Isaiah 14.[35] That unnamed king arrogantly "said in [his] heart, 'I will ascend to the heavens; . . . above the stars of God; . . . I will ascend above the tops of the clouds; I will make myself like the Most High'" (vv. 13-14). In the time of first-century AD Rome, in a vision parallel to Daniel's, the apostle John "saw a beast coming out of the sea" (Rev. 13:1). This beast, too, "was given a [human-like] mouth," which he used "to blaspheme God, and to slander his name and his dwelling place and those who live in heaven" (vv. 5-6).

Second, this last king in Daniel's vision will "oppress the saints of the Most High" (Dan. 7:25, AT). The Aramaic word for "oppress" literally means "to wear away" and is used here figuratively for "harass continually."[36]

---

34. Edlin, *Daniel*, 185.
35. Goldingay, *Daniel*, 391.
36. Brown, Driver, and Briggs, *Hebrew and English Lexicon*, 1080.

Thus it indicates that this fourth "king's attacks upon the faithful will be relentless."[37] Stephen Miller opines that "believers will daily be harassed until their lives become miserable. Religious freedom will be abolished (cf. 9:27), and economic pressure will be applied to force his subjects to follow him and reject religion (cf. Rev 13:16-17)."[38]

Third, this last king in Daniel's vision will "try to change the set times and the laws" (Dan. 7:25). Edlin suggests that these most likely refer "to prescribed worship practices outlined in the laws of Moses. These include such things as Sabbath observance, sacrifice rituals, and annual festivals."[39]

But the oppressive rule of this last king of Daniel's vision will not continue forever. The angelic interpreter promises, "They [i.e., God's saints] will be given into his hand for [only] a time, times, and half a time" (v. 25, AT). This king will indeed have control of history for some time, but his control will end, even if he thinks it won't. There is someone far greater who truly has control.[40]

So the same court that Daniel saw in the early scene of his vision again will sit to pass judgment on this last king. There will be no long deliberations, no calling of endless witnesses, no recesses or appeals. One assumes the Superior Judge to be the Ancient of Days, who took his courtroom or throneroom seat in verse 9 and who gave a judgment in favor of his embattled saints in verse 22. The verdict will be that the last king's "power [*šālṭān*] will be taken away and completely destroyed forever" (v. 26). This "power [*šālṭān*] will be given to the saints of the Most High" (v. 27, AT). That is, all those belonging to the Most High will be his subjects in "his kingdom," sharing in the "power and greatness of all the kingdoms under heaven" (v. 27). In other words, all earthly kingdoms will now be absorbed under the one "everlasting kingdom" ruled by God Most High (v. 27). In this kingdom, all rulers (and all peoples) "will worship and obey him" (v. 27).

---

37. Edlin, *Daniel*, 186.
38. Miller, *Daniel*, 214.
39. Edlin, *Daniel*, 186.
40. Goldingay, *Daniel*, 391.

Finally, Daniel added an addendum to the narrator's account of his night dream vision, that this experience left him deeply troubled of mind. Yet, he said, "I kept the matter to myself" (v. 28), which, of course, he didn't!

Customs and Practices Explained

Daniel's "Four Winds of Heaven" (Dan. 7:2)

In addition to using this expression in 7:2, Daniel also used it in 8:8 and 11:4. He did not use this expression in biblical cultural isolation, however, for the "four winds of heaven" and similar expressions of the "winds" occur frequently in Mesopotamian and Egyptian texts—the Old Testament's wider cultural context. In these texts, the "four winds" are associated with the four cardinal directions—north, south, east, and west. Sometimes these winds have wings, or the wind and wing are identified as identical. At other times, these winds and wings are perceived as bearing the flights of the various deities, and in Israelite theology, the flight or travel of Yahweh and his chariot.

In Mesopotamian Akkadian, there is a word that means "circle, loop, circumference, and totality," and when applied to "the earth or the winds, it represents all directions, i.e., everywhere the winds blow." The Mesopotamian storm god Adad is said to possess the "circle of the four winds."[41]

In Egypt, in one theology, the four winds are personified as winged beings and represent the four cardinal directions. It is said that these four winds united to divide earth from heaven and thus created the universe.[42]

In the Old Testament, the psalmist of Psalm 104 graphically describes the "LORD" (Yahweh) "designating the clouds his chariot, cruising upon the wings of the wind" (vv. 2-3, AT), then making those very "winds" (plural) to be "his messengers," "his servants" (v. 4), as he (Yahweh) carries out his creation of the earth and the universe. The psalmist very descriptively details this creation process in verses 5-35. One might speculate that the psalmist

---

41. Scott B. Noegel, "On the Wings of the Winds: Towards an Understanding of Winged *Mischwesen* in the Ancient Near East," *Kaskal: A Journal of History, Environments, and Cultures of the Ancient Near East* 14 (2017): 17.
42. Ibid., 17-19.

may have been aware of the Egyptian theology of the winds as creator and is doing a one-upmanship here! The "winds" did *not* create. Only the "Lord" (Yahweh) is creator of all that is!

Royal Record Keeping ("The Books Were Opened" [Dan. 7:10*c*])

In the nations and empires of the ancient Near East, official records were kept of happenings in the king's domain and of royal decisions and edicts. These records were archived in the palace of an empire's capital city, such as Nineveh or Babylon, or in the palace of a large city-state, such as Ugarit or Ebla. Some of these have been discovered, read, and published in modern times.

Ezra 4:15 refers to official "archives" or "records" of events that happened during the reigns of Persian king Artaxerxes's "predecessors" (lit. "[fore] fathers"). Esther 6:1 tells us that one night when Persian king Xerxes had insomnia, he called for "the book of the chronicles [lit. "memorials"], the record of his reign, to be brought in and read to him."

Punishment by Burning (Dan. 7:11)

The literature of the Babylonian, Persian, and Greek periods witness to the practice of burning by fire as punishment for crimes.[43] In Jeremiah 29:21-23, Jeremiah witnesses to the practice in Babylon when he speaks of Zedekiah and Ahab, two Judean false prophets among the early exiles in Babylon, whom Nebuchadnezzar king of Babylon "burned [lit. "roasted" (*klh*)] in the fire" (v. 22). What crime they had committed against the king to warrant such punishment Jeremiah does not say. Their crime against Yahweh, however, for which he gave them into the king's hand, was prophesying lies in Yahweh's name and committing adultery with the wives of their neighbors.

That punishment by burning was practiced during Babylonian Nebuchadnezzar's time is further corroborated by the threat of Daniel 3:6. There,

---

43. Goldingay, *Daniel*, 233.

anyone who would not worship the king's golden image would "immediately be thrown into a blazing furnace."

Elsewhere in the Old Testament, burning by fire was an acceptable punishment for a serious offense or crime, as indicated in Genesis 38:24; Leviticus 20:14; 21:9; and Joshua 7:15, 25. Metaphorically, fire was an acceptable divine punishment as indicated in Isaiah 30:33; Ezekiel 28:18; 38:22; and Psalm 11:6.

In the Greek period, the seventh chapter of the Jewish book 2 Maccabees (second century BC) details the martyrdom of the seven brothers and their mother at the hands of the Seleucid king Antiochus. Their crime? Refusal "to partake of unlawful swine's flesh" (v. 1, NRSV).[44] Antiochus did not actually burn these victims in the fire itself, however. Rather, he first horribly tortured them, one after the other, and then, while they were still alive, fried each of them in pans heated to high heat over fire (see vv. 3-5).

God behind the Scenes

In vision one (Dan. 7), God, identified as the Ancient of Days, is both active behind and within the scenes as Daniel 7 unfolds. He is seated on a royal throne in a throne room specifically set up to function as a courtroom (vv. 9-10). God's first act in this capacity was to pass judgment on the four beasts of Daniel's vision (vv. 11-12). God's second act of rendering justice, still identified as the Ancient of Days, was to judge in favor of the "saints of the Most High" (*qaddîšê 'elyônîn*, AT) in a war in which the fourth beast (small horn) was defeated (v. 22). Thus, in Daniel 7, God, the Supreme Judge, defeated and destroyed the wicked of this earth, while saving and elevating the saints who serve God.

In another Old Testament text, David speaks of God acting similarly as earth's Supreme Judge. In Psalm 58, David challenges earthly "rulers" (v. 1 [2 HB]): "Do you judge humankind [lit. "sons of man" (*běnê 'ādām*; NIV:

44. Howard Clark Kee, ed., *Cambridge Annotated Study Apocrypha: New Revised Standard Version* (Cambridge, UK: Cambridge University, 1994), 164-66.

"people")] fairly? Indeed not! In your heart you commit injustice; [then] on the earth your hands deal out [lit. "weigh out"] violence" (vv. 1-2 [2-3 HB], AT). The evilness of these wicked rulers or judges is in their very nature; it is with them "even from birth [from the womb]," says David. They spend their lives "spreading lies" (v. 3 [4 HB]).

Yet David envisions hope for "the righteous [who] will rejoice when they see vengeance" (v. 10a [11a HB], AT). The designation the "righteous" (ṣadîq) here in Psalm 58:10a (v. 11a HB) is equivalent to the "saints of the Most High" (qaddîšê 'elyônîn) in Daniel 7:22 (AT). Both are the true followers of God.

In his conclusion of Psalm 58 David declares, "Then humanity ['ādām] will say, 'Surely [Indeed]! There is a reward for the righteous [laṣṣadîq]'" (v. 11a [12a HB], AT). Allen Ross clarifies that "the 'righteous' is singular in form, but collective in meaning."[45]

David then adds his capstone statement, "Surely [Indeed]! There is a God who judges in the earth" (v. 11b [12b HB], AT). The implication here is that in contrast to those earthly rulers who judge humanity unrighteously (vv. 1-2 [2-3 HB]), God judges with righteous impartiality. Ross says that the word "judges" in Psalm 58:11b (v. 12b HB), in reference to God, "refers to his whole administration or governing of the earth and not just the destruction of the wicked who do not think there is a higher power over the affairs of man."[46]

The Vision's Relationship, If Any, to the Other Three Visions or Previous Six Stories

There is *a uniqueness* to vision one (Dan. 7). Both Jim Edlin and J. Paul Tanner view Daniel 7 functioning as a "hinge" chapter between the two divisions of Daniel, chapters 1–6 and 7–12. By "hinge" they mean that

---

45. Allen P. Ross, *A Commentary on the Psalms: Volume 2 (42–89)* (Grand Rapids: Kregel, 2013), 312.
46. Ibid., 313.

Daniel 7 functions as both a conclusion to the court tales (first division) and an introduction to the visions (second division).[47]

As a *conclusion* to the first division, one obvious connection is the two dreams of four world kingdoms in both chapters 2 and 7. In Nebuchadnezzar's dream of chapter 2, the statue depicts these kingdoms "from a human standpoint," while in Daniel's dream of chapter 7, the beasts depict the "kingdoms from God's point of view."[48]

As an *introduction* to the second division, chapter 7 introduces a "new genre, the apocalyptic styled vision report," which will continue into the following chapters.[49] These visions will use symbolic animals and symbolic numbers; heavenly beings will appear to explain the visions.[50] Of note also is the little horn (lit. "another horn, a little one") in verse 8, which emerges from the fourth beast mentioned in verse 7. Christian interpreters down through history have associated this little horn with the antichrist, an end-time figure who opposes both God and God's people. This figure of opposition will continue throughout Daniel 7–12.[51]

The Antichrist in the New Testament

New Testament writers seem to have had in the background Daniel's antichrist when speaking of rebellious persons as "false messiahs" (Mark 13:22), "the man of lawlessness" and "the lawless one" (2 Thess. 2:3, 8-9), "the antichrist" (1 John 2:18, 22; 4:3; 2 John 7), and "the beast" (Rev. 13:1-6, 8).

---

47. Edlin, *Daniel*, 168; Tanner, *Daniel*, 29, 30.
48. Edlin, *Daniel*, 169.
49. Ibid.
50. Ibid.
51. Ibid., 189; Tanner, *Daniel*, 34.

Faithful Living Today

There are many in political leadership or rulership in today's world who do not recognize any power higher than themselves or their ruling regimes. Followers of biblical faith seeking to live according to the teachings of our Lord Jesus Christ, who must live under the authority of these leaders or rulers, often have little or no freedom to do so. We see our freedoms to teach others and to live out these teachings openly being restricted in our Western nations currently at a pace many of us have never before experienced. Yet we can and must live in faith that the Most High God is indeed in control, and ultimately every earthly ruler and vaunted kingdom "will worship and obey him" (Dan. 7:27).

13

Vision Two (Dan. 8)

Summary

In Daniel 8 we read of Daniel's second vision in which he saw a ram with two horns and a shaggy goat with a single horn between its eyes, which was replaced with four horns (vv. 3, 5, 8). The ram represented the kings of Media and Persia (v. 20). The shaggy goat represented Greece: its single large horn represented the first conquering king of Greece and his empire, while the four horns that replaced the large horn represented four kingdoms into which the king's empire divided after his death (vv. 21-22).

The interpreter of this vision for Daniel was the angel Gabriel, who suddenly stood before him (vv. 15-16). Daniel was so astonished to be in the presence of such an august person, he fell prostrate to the ground (v. 17). While facedown on the ground, Daniel passed into a trance. With a touch, however, Gabriel raised him up (v. 18).

Though Gabriel gave Daniel the vision's interpretation, he told him that the world events in that interpretation were to take place in the "distant future" (v. 26). That is, none of the events of this vision would happen in Daniel's lifetime.

The Vision

Daniel narrated this vision in first person speech, which, he said, appeared to him after he had received an earlier vision (Dan. 8:1). That earlier first vision was most surely the vision of Daniel 7, which he had also narrated in first person speech. This current second vision of Daniel 8 occurred during King Belshazzar's third year of reign (v. 1), which was about 548 or 547 BC.[1] (The earlier vision of Dan. 7 occurred in King Belshazzar's first year of reign [v. 1], which was about 550 or 549 BC.)

When this second vision came to him, Daniel was in "the citadel of Susa" (8:2), some two hundred miles east of Babylon, in the province of Elam. "Citadel" is bîrâ, meaning "fortress." Susa, therefore, was a fortified city, of significant power in earlier times. In 640 BC, however, Assyrian king Ashurbanipal conquered Elam, destroying Susa. More specifically, Daniel was by a "canal [or tributary] of the Ulay River" (v. 2).[2] In one of his inscriptions, Ashurbanipal used the phrase "within Ulayan Susa." By this he was "referring to the entire district around Susa, with its numerous smaller streams and canals."[3]

Was Daniel physically present in Susa at the time this vision came to him? The text does not specify, though several scholars assume the text to be depicting a visionary experience or journey only.[4]

Whether present in Susa physically or only through a visionary experience, why *Susa*, if it was a destroyed city? Perhaps the vision intended to signal that Susa was soon to regain its importance.[5] Not so very long after Daniel's vision, Persian king Darius I (r. 522–486 BC) would rebuild and establish Susa as one of the capitals of the Persian Empire.

The vision of Daniel 8 and its interpretation will be viewed in *five scenes*.

---

1. Gerhard F. Hasel, "The First and Third Years of Belshazzar (Daniel 7:1; 8:1)," *Andrews University Seminary Studies* 15, no. 2 (1977): 162, 168.

2. J. J. Finkelstein, "Mesopotamia," *Journal of Near Eastern Studies* 21, no. 2 (1962): 89.

3. Ibid.

4. For example, Goldingay, *Daniel*, 419; Lucas, *Daniel*, 212.

5. Tanner, *Daniel*, 485.

Scene One (Dan. 8:3-4)

Daniel first saw a ram (male sheep) "standing beside the canal" (v. 3). It had two horns of unequal length, with the shorter one eventually growing to become the longer. This ram was charging about to the west, north, and south, ramming all other animals in its path. Seemingly, none could stand before "its power," since it "did as it pleased" (v. 4). Some ancient Greek and Hebrew manuscripts of Daniel, for various reasons uneasy with the omission of the fourth compass point, have added east. But Jim Edlin aptly suggests that the omission of east from the Masoretic Text "seems to indicate that the ram came out of the east."[6] (See my discussion of v. 20 below, p. 160.)

Scene Two (Dan. 8:5-8)

The two-horned ram's power and rampaging, however, in terms of history's time span, was short lived. The scene suddenly changed to reveal a male goat advancing from the direction of the west. Between its eyes it had a "prominent horn" (v. 5). This male goat appeared to be flying, since it did not touch the ground as it passed over the entire earth (much like the mythical Rudolph and his flying reindeer team!) (v. 5).

With furious rage, this male goat attacked the unsuspecting two-horned ram. It shattered both the ram's horns, knocked it down, and trampled it underfoot (vv. 6-7). Daniel did not say where this vicious fight took place.

But at the height of the male goat's power, its prominent horn was broken off. As Daniel continued watching in his vision, in place of this prominent horn, there emerged four other prominent horns. Their political and military control, in turn, extended "toward the four winds of heaven," that is, in all the four cardinal directions—north, south, east, and west (v. 8). (See my discussion at vv. 21-22, pp. 160-61.)

---

6. Edlin, *Daniel*, 199.

Scene Three (Dan. 8:9-12)

The scene in Daniel's vision changed again. From one of the four prominent horns of the previous scene, a little horn emerged (this was *not* the same as the little horn of Dan. 7:8). It increased exceedingly (militarily and politically is implied), however, southward and eastward and toward "the beauty" (*haṣṣebî*; AT) or "the fairest"[7] (8:9). The New International Version's "the Beautiful Land" here is apparently influenced by 11:16 and 41, where the angel Gabriel spoke of "the Beautiful Land" (*'ereṣ haṣṣĕbî*) (in the context there, referring to Judea). Edlin suggests that "*the beauty* (*haṣṣebî*) [of 8:9] is a reference either to Judah, Jerusalem, or the temple area in particular."[8] (See the sidebar "The Hebrew Term *ṣĕbî*" below.)

The Hebrew Term *ṣĕbî*

The term *ṣĕbî* means "glory," "beauty," "honor," or "splendor."[9] Ezekiel twice applied this term to the land the "LORD" (Yahweh) had chosen for his people Israel even before bringing them out of Egypt. He describes this land (Canaan) as "the most beautiful [*ṣĕbî*] of all lands" and linked this beauty with the land's products: "a land flowing with milk and honey" (Ezek. 20:6, 15). In Daniel 11:45, the one earlier described as "dressed in linen" (10:5) called the temple mount "the beautiful [*ṣĕbî*] holy mountain."

In this vision two, Daniel watched as the military and political power of this small horn increased, both geographically and, metaphorically, heavenward "as far as the host of heaven" (*'ad ṣĕbā' haššāmāyim*; v. 10, AT). It caused some of that heavenly host (Daniel speaks of them symbolically as "stars" [*hakkôkābîm*; AT]) to fall earthward, where it "trampled" them underfoot (v. 10).

---

7. Goldingay, *Daniel*, 402, 421.
8. Edlin, *Daniel*, 200 (italics original).
9. Brown, Driver, and Briggs, *Hebrew and English Lexicon*, 840; *Dictionary of Classical Hebrew*, 7:70; Koehler, Baumgartner, and Stamm, *Hebrew and Aramaic Lexicon*, 3998.

In a later discussion, we will see that the small horn here of verses 9-12 is the same as the "fierce-looking king" of verses 23-25. That king represents Antiochus Epiphanes IV, who ruled the Greek Seleucid Kingdom from 176 to 164 BC, perpetrating terrible sufferings on the Jewish people of Judea. Some of these sufferings, as recorded in the book of 1 Maccabees, will be noted later.

Here in Daniel 8, the small horn (Antiochus Epiphanes IV) challenged the "Prince of the [heavenly] host" (*śar haṣṣābā'*) with an extremely sacrilegious act: "he took away [lit. "lifted up"] the daily sacrifice" so that "the place of *his* sanctuary [*mĕkôn miqdāšô*] was overthrown" (v. 11, AT; emphasis added). The pronoun "his" refers to the "Prince," who surely is God, and his "sanctuary" surely refers to the Jerusalem temple, which Jewish returnees from Babylonian captivity had rebuilt in the sixth century BC.

Antiochus Epiphanes IV's act of sacrilege was to deny the Jews living in Jerusalem in the second century BC the freedom to offer the daily sacrifices. These were the whole burnt offerings offered every morning and evening in the Jerusalem temple.

Thus, in the time of the small horn (Antiochus Epiphanes IV) in the second century BC, without these regular sacrifices, "his [i.e., God's] sanctuary was overthrown" (v. 11, AT). This did not mean that the temple was physically destroyed but rather became a place where no longer "Israel's God [could be] appropriately honored."[10]

This small horn, moreover, treated "truth" as nothing but something to be "thrown to the ground" (v. 12). During all this, the small horn seemingly "prospered in everything it did" (v. 12). Tragically, God's people, Daniel says, having no choice, were "given over" to all this oppression (v. 12). "Given over" implies that God allowed all this to happen, that his divine hand was still in control.[11] Thus the outcome of these circumstances would be controlled by God, not by the little, arrogant horn! (For a discussion of the

10. Edlin, *Daniel*, 201.
11. Ibid., 202.

atrocities the little horn [Antiochus Epiphanes IV] perpetrated against God's people, see the discussion of vv. 23-25 below, pp. 161-62.)

Scene Four (Dan. 8:13-14)

Daniel now reported that he (over)heard two holy ones speaking with each other, who were probably heavenly beings. They seem to have been discussing the meaning of Daniel's vision,[12] but Daniel reported only the end of their conversation.

Daniel heard one of these holy ones speaking but doesn't report what he was saying. Then another holy one breaks in, asking the first one how long it would take for the events Daniel had seen in this vision to be completed (v. 13). In the upcoming discussion of verses 23-25, as already noted above, the arrogant little horn is to be identified with the "fierce-looking king" of verse 23, who is to be identified with Antiochus Epiphanes IV (r. 176-164 BC), who perpetrated terrible sufferings on the Jewish people of Judea. Thus the holy one here is asking, When will the suffering of God's people at the hands of this cruel king come to an end? When will the daily sacrifice at the Jerusalem temple be restored? When will Antiochus's appalling rebellion against God be crushed? When will the people of God cease to be trampled underfoot? (v. 13).

It is not clear which holy one responded to the question. Daniel says, "Then he said to me" (v. 14, AT). One assumes it was the first holy one he heard speaking. The response was, "Until 2,300 evenings and mornings"; at the end of this period, "the sanctuary"—that is, the Jerusalem temple—"will be set right" (v. 14, AT).

The period of 2,300 evenings and mornings has been an enigma for commentators. Some suggest that 2,300 refers to 2,300 daily sacrifices—that is, 2 per day (morning and evening), thus 1,150 days, or, as in Genesis 1:5, "morning and evening" equals one day, thus 2,300 days. The date often put forward for the ending of the suffering of God's people perpetrated by

---

12. Goldingay, *Daniel*, 423.

Antiochus Epiphanes IV is December 164 BC, when Judas Maccabeus and his brothers cleansed the Jerusalem temple, rebuilt the altar, and restarted the daily burnt offering (1 Macc. 4:36-58). Still, no one has devised a calculation that fits all the historical data. Edlin suggests that "the number appears to be symbolic as are most numbers in the book of Daniel,"[13] while Goldingay says that the number is probably just referring to "a 'significant' period."[14]

Scene Five (Dan. 8:15-26)

Though this scene overall gives the interpretation of Daniel's vision, we may view it in three subunits: (1) a conversation between two heavenly beings (vv. 15-16); (2) Daniel's reaction to the presence of Gabriel, one of the heavenly beings (vv. 17-18); and (3) Gabriel's interpretation of Daniel's vision (vv. 19-26).

Subunit One (Dan. 8:15-16)

The kaleidoscopic parade of visionary scenes recounted in verses 2-14 has ceased. Daniel now remarks that while viewing this vision and seeking an understanding of it, he saw a being suddenly standing before him whose appearance was like that of a "man" (v. 15). The word for "man" here is the Hebrew term *geber* (significantly, not *'ādām*, the generic term for "mankind"). *Geber* is a very masculine term.[15] This concept is expressed in Yahweh's command to Job in Job 38:3: "Brace yourself like a man [*kĕgeber*]; I will question you, and you shall answer me." The term also describes a "man" in his close relationship with and dependence on God, as noted in Jeremiah 17:7: "Blessed is the man [*haggeber*] who trusts in the LORD [*yhwh*]; indeed, the LORD [*yhwh*] being his trust" (AT).

Daniel then heard a voice calling out, which he describes as a human voice, but of someone who was not visible. This voice called to the person standing in front of Daniel, with this command: "Gabriel, interpret for this

---

13. Edlin, *Daniel*, 203.
14. Goldingay, *Daniel*, 426.
15. See ibid.

man the vision!" (v. 16, AT). Who is the one giving this command? Edlin says that it is unclear from the text. Thus it may be God or an angel, but "in any case the ultimate authority behind such a voice is God."[16] Goldingay unequivocally opts for the voice belonging to God.[17] Tanner suggests that the person behind the voice "may be the preincarnate Lord Jesus Christ."[18] From this voice's command, however, we learn that the name of the man-like person in front of Daniel is Gabriel, in Hebrew *gabrî'ēl*. The first three consonants of this name are *gbr*, the same as the three consonants in *geber*, "man." The last part in the name is *'ēl*, meaning "God." Thus Gabriel means "man of God." Thus Gabriel is a heavenly being, an angel, one of God's special agents, with an intimate and special relationship to God, the highest being in all creation.

Subunit Two (Dan. 8:17-18)

As the angel Gabriel approached Daniel, Daniel became so "terrified" (*bā'at*; a Hebrew word that expresses "the terror of a lesser individual who stands in the presence of a greater individual")[19] that he fell facedown on the ground. While still in that position, Daniel fell into a trance; yet he still heard, and later remembered, that Gabriel told him that the vision's main focus concerned the "time of the end [*qēṣ*]" (see the discussion of "end" [*qēṣ*] at v. 19 below). Gabriel then touched Daniel and enabled him to stand.

Subunit Three (Dan. 8:19-26)

Gabriel then told Daniel "what will happen during the latter time of the wrath [*hazzā'am*], because at a set moment there will be an end [*qēṣ*]" (v. 19, AT). There are several differing scholarly understandings of the meaning of "the time of wrath." Of the more likely (in my view), two deserve mention: (1) that it refers to the period beginning with the fall of Jerusalem in 587 BC to the end of Antiochus Epiphanes IV's persecution in the mid-second

---

16. Edlin, *Daniel*, 204.
17. Goldingay, *Daniel*, 427.
18. Tanner, *Daniel*, 507.
19. *New International Dictionary of Old Testament*, 1:680.

century BC[20] or (2) that it refers to the shorter period of persecution that the little horn perpetrated upon the Jews, as detailed in Daniel 8:8-13 and 23-25, and was fulfilled by the persecution and human devastation of Antiochus Epiphanes IV.[21] I am partial toward this second interpretation. Moreover, there is a divinely appointed terminal point at which the persecution of Antiochus Epiphanes IV will end. This is what is meant by "an end" (*qēṣ*) in verse 19, not the final end of human history.[22]

In verse 20, Gabriel mentioned the two-horned ram that Daniel had seen earlier in this vision. There, Daniel had noted that the two horns were of unequal length (vv. 3-4). Now, Gabriel gave the ram's interpretation: it, or rather its two horns, "represents the kings of Media and Persia" (v. 20). Historically, in the early period of these two kingdoms, the Median Kingdom (at first the longer horn) was stronger than the Persian Kingdom (the shorter horn). In 612 BC, while still the stronger, the Medes joined the Babylonians to defeat the Assyrians. They then merged with the Babylonians.

Also earlier in this vision, Daniel had watched as this two-horned ram "gored" (AT) (NIV: "charged") westward, northward, and southward (see v. 4). Significantly, it did not gore eastward. Perhaps this goring represents the Median and Persian combined military actions that occurred (1) in 546 BC, in which they took over the northern kingdom of Lydia (in present-day Turkey); (2) in 539 BC, in which their armies advanced westward to conquer Babylon; and (3) in 525 BC, now primarily Persian armies, which expanded southward, conquering Egypt.

Subsequently, the shorter horn grew to be longer. Representing Persian power, it expanded eastward to the western border of India. In time, the Persian Empire became the largest empire the world had yet known.

In verse 21, Gabriel spoke of the male shaggy goat that Daniel had seen earlier in this vision (vv. 5-8). He said that this goat represents the king of Greece,

20. Goldingay, *Daniel*, 428.
21. Edlin, *Daniel*, 206.
22. Goldingay, *Daniel*, 429.

and the horn between its eyes is the first king. Historically, the first king of a united Greece was Alexander the Great (r. 356-323 BC). He is the flying goat of 8:5, for with great speed he came eastward from Greece in the west, conquering the entire Persian Empire in only three years (334-331 BC), expanding his Greek Empire all the way eastward to the western border of India.

In verse 22, Gabriel spoke of the shaggy goat's horn that Daniel earlier saw broken off and replaced by four other horns (v. 8). The horn that was broken off represents the untimely death of Alexander the Great in 323 BC at the young age of thirty-two. Though historians debate the cause of his death, perhaps the most credible is that while stopping in Babylon on his return from India, one night he and some of his men had been doing some heavy drinking. Thus "severe alcohol poisoning" combined with a fever may have caused his death.[23]

The four horns that replaced the horn that was broken off are four kingdoms arising from the single nation of the king of Greece, but with reduced power. Historians understand these to represent the four Greek kingdoms into which Alexander's vast empire divided, each headed by one of Alexander's generals. These were (1) Thrace and Bithynia under Lysimachus; (2) Macedon and Greece under Cassander; (3) Syria, Babylonia, and Mesopotamia under Seleucus; and (4) Egypt, Judah, and Arabia under Ptolemy.

In verses 23-25, Gabriel said of one of these four kingdoms, "A fierce-looking king, a master of intrigue, will arise" (v. 23). He will use his power to "destroy . . . the holy people" (v. 24). Moreover, he will challenge the authority of the "Prince of princes," that is, God (v. 25). This "fierce-looking" despot is most surely the little horn of verses 8-12. Most biblical commentators and historians identify this person as the Greek Seleucid king Antiochus Epiphanes IV, who ruled the Seleucid Kingdom from 175 to 164 BC and whose kingdom included Judah.

---

23. Tanner, *Daniel*, 489.

Antiochus IV gave himself the additional name Epiphanes, meaning "Illustrious" or "Shining One," and thus he is known in history as Antiochus Epiphanes IV. He committed unspeakable crimes against the Jews and the Jewish faith. In the seven-year period from 171 to 164 BC, at his orders, thousands of Jews died. The little horn's throwing truth to the ground (see v. 12) may refer to Antiochus Epiphanes IV's literal tearing to pieces of the Jewish "books of the law" and burning them (1 Macc. 1:56, NRSV). In December 167 BC, he erected an altar to the Greek deity Zeus in the Jerusalem temple courts and sacrificed swine on it. (See the sidebar "Antiochus Epiphanes IV's Acts of Sacrilege, as Recorded in 1 Maccabees 1," p. 163.) In Greek mythology, Zeus was considered to be "the supreme deity, ruler of gods and humanity, . . . identified as 'Father.' . . . From Zeus emanated all revelation."[24] His act of erecting this altar to Zeus was Antiochus IV's ultimate challenge to the Jewish belief in the supremacy of God, the "Prince of princes" (Dan. 8:25).

Gabriel now gave a word of comfort, though Daniel didn't have a clue as to whom these concluding remarks were pointing (see v. 27): "Yet, without (human) power, he will be broken" (v. 25, AT). "He" is Antiochus Epiphanes IV. This was a prophetic word of comfort intended for God's people far in the future.

In verse 26, Daniel recorded Gabriel's final comment concerning his vision. Gabriel first reaffirmed the validity of the vision: "The vision of the evenings and the mornings is reliable [ʾĕmet]" (AT). By mentioning "the evenings and the mornings," Gabriel was saying that the vision's focus points toward a future time when Antiochus Epiphanes IV will prevent the Jews from offering the daily morning and evening sacrifices at the Jerusalem temple. (See the discussion of vv. 23-25 above and the sidebar "Antiochus Epiphanes IV's Acts of Sacrilege, as Recorded in 1 Maccabees 1," on the following page.)

---

24. *International Standard Bible Encyclopedia*, 4:1194.

Finally, Gabriel commanded Daniel, "But, you—seal up the vision because [it is] for many days [from now]!" (v. 26, AT). Thus the historical outworking of the details of this vision would not take place within Daniel's lifetime. Implied was that Daniel was to write on a scroll the details of this vision for future readers. "It must be kept safe in order to preserve it from corruption and to ensure its availability for the time to which it applies."[25]

Conclusion (Dan. 8:27)

Daniel's experience of this vision and encounter with Gabriel left him exhausted and ill for several days. He recovered, however, and was able to arise from his sickbed and perform the duties of his employment in service to the king (Belshazzar [v. 1]). Yet he did not understand the meaning and implications of his vision.

Antiochus Epiphanes IV's Acts of Sacrilege, as Recorded in 1 Maccabees 1

Two passages from 1 Maccabees 1 partially tell the story. The first, verses 44-47, reads,

And the king [Antiochus Epiphanes IV] sent letters by messengers to Jerusalem and the towns of Judah; he directed them to follow customs strange to the land, to forbid burnt offerings and sacrifices and drink offerings in the sanctuary, to profane sabbaths and festivals, to defile the sanctuary and the priests, to build altars and sacred precincts and shrines for idols, to sacrifice swine and other unclean animals.

The second, verses 54-59, reads,

Now on the fifteenth day of Chislev in the one hundred forty-fifth year, they erected a desolating sacrilege on the altar of burnt offering. They also built altars in the surrounding towns of Judah, and offered incense at the doors of the houses and in the streets. The books of the law that they found they tore to pieces and burned with fire. . . . On

---

25. Edlin, *Daniel*, 210.

the twenty-fifth day of the month they offered sacrifice on the altar that was on top of the altar of burnt offering.[26]

Customs and Practices Explained

The Daily (Morning and Evening) Sacrifices (Dan. 8:11)

Antiochus Epiphanes IV "took away the daily sacrifice" from the Jerusalem temple (v. 11). God had first commanded that his people offer these in the wilderness tabernacle (Exod. 29:38-42; Num. 28:2-9). Later, they continued to offer them in Solomon's temple. They could not offer them, however, after the Babylonians destroyed Solomon's temple in 587 BC. But at the time of Zerubbabel's rebuilding the temple in the sixth century BC, even before laying the foundation of the temple itself, the people built an altar and resumed offering the morning and evening sacrifices (Ezra 3:2-6).

Sealed Documents (Dan. 8:26)

Gabriel commanded Daniel to seal up the vision that he had seen and Gabriel had interpreted. This implies that it must first be written on a scroll. The scroll is then tied up with a string. A blob of wet clay is then attached to the tie of the string into which the author or owner impresses his or her personal seal. The clay then hardens, becoming the "seal" of the scroll. Sometimes the scroll is then placed in a clay container or jar for preservation. An example of this process is found in Jeremiah 32:9-15. Jeremiah purchased a field from his cousin. The terms of purchase were written on a deed, with a copy made, the original of which Jeremiah signed and sealed and had witnesses also sign. He then directed that both the sealed and unsealed copies be placed "in a clay jar so they will last a long time" (v. 14).

---

26. Howard Clark Kee, ed., *Cambridge Annotated Study Apocrypha: New Revised Standard Version* (Cambridge, UK: Cambridge University, 1994), 128-29.

God behind the Scenes

God is not mentioned throughout vision two (Dan. 8) except by the title "Prince of princes" (v. 25). It is against the "Prince of princes" that Antiochus Epiphanes IV will vaunt himself. "Yet he will be destroyed," Gabriel said, "but not by human power" (v. 25). Implied is that it will be God's power that breaks him! According to 1 Maccabees 6:5-16, Antiochus did not die a warrior's death in battle. It seems that after he had failed in an attempt to rob the temple of Nanaea in Elymais (located in ancient Persia [modern Iran]), he was informed that the Jews had risen up and defeated his forces in Judea. He died perhaps of insanity or at least of severe depression.

The Vision's Relationship, If Any, to the Other Three Visions or Previous Six Stories

Vision two (Dan. 8) is related back to vision one (Dan. 7) and forward to the three visions of Daniel 9–12.

Jim Edlin gives the essential relationships as follows: Daniel saw the visions of both *chapters 7 and 8* during Belshazzar's reign (first and third years). In both, animals represent human kingdoms and horns symbolize rulers, while a small horn points to a ruler who oppresses God's people. As for *chapters 9–12*, along with *chapter 8*, the visions "in these chapters each climax with a critical event when the sacrifice in the temple ceases . . . (8:10-13; 9:27; 11:31; 12:11). In each case a time limit regarding the duration of this crisis is announced (8:14; 9:24-27; 11:33-35; 12:11-12)."[27]

Faithful Living Today

Though we who live in North America do not live under the rule of evil tyrants (though some may act in such a manner), others in many parts of our world do! The final message of vision two (Dan. 8) is "that God remains in

---

27. Edlin, *Daniel*, 193-94.

control and determines the end of evil tyrants."[28] The example given in this vision is that of Antiochus Epiphanes IV. Although Antiochus was a tyrant magnified many times over, he was broken by God, the Prince of princes, who is still on his throne today. We can live assured that God has not abandoned us, his beloved people!

28. Ibid., 213.

14

Vision Three (Dan. 9)

Summary

Daniel's vision three (Dan. 9) occurred in the first year of Persian king Darius's reign (v. 1). It was not all vision, however.

In verses 3-19, Daniel prayed a prayer to the "LORD my God" on behalf of the Jews of Judah, Jerusalem, and all Israel (v. 4). In his prayer, he confessed to God that in the past "we have . . . rebelled" against "your commands and laws" (v. 5). This was the reason, Daniel said, that you, God, brought upon us the great disaster of the loss of "Jerusalem, your city, your holy hill" (v. 16). Coupled with his request to God, Daniel pled for the restoration of Jerusalem: "Because of your great mercy . . . Lord, forgive! . . . For your sake, my God, do not delay" (vv. 18-19).

In verses 20-27, Daniel told of this vision that came while he was still praying. The man Gabriel, whom he had seen in a previous vision, showed up with a message. Though Gabriel did not mention God or heaven, the implication was that because Daniel was "highly esteemed," heaven had been listening from the moment he began to pray (v. 23). In response, God had sent a word (a vision) to Daniel, and Gabriel was the follow-up person to make its meaning known to him. The vision would involve a period of time described as "Seventy 'sevens'" (v. 24). This period will bracket the initiation of the rebuilding of Jerusalem and the death of an anointed person. The vision concluded with the depiction of war and desolations.

The Prayer and the Vision

Daniel's Prayer (Dan. 9:1-19)

Daniel prayed this prayer sometime in 539-538 BC, during Darius the Mede's first year of reign in Babylon (v. 1). Darius the Mede should not be confused with the later Darius (whom scholars call Darius I or Darius the Great) who ruled from 522 to 486 BC. Rather, Darius the Mede is the Darius-Cyrus who captured Babylon in 539 BC from Belshazzar (see the sidebar "Who Was Darius the Mede?" in section titled "The Sixth Story [Dan. 6]," in ch. 4, "Chapter Summaries," p. 32).

It seems that Daniel had been reading/studying "the documents" (Dan. 9:2, AT; NIV: "the Scriptures"). Among them was a manuscript containing all, or at least some, of the writings of the earlier Judean prophet Jeremiah. Daniel described these writings as the "word of the LORD" (*děbar yhwh*; v. 2). In this document, Daniel noticed that Jeremiah had prophesied "that the desolation of Jerusalem would last seventy years" (v. 2). Moreover, Jeremiah had mentioned this time period *twice* in his manuscript. The first, Jeremiah 25:1-11, was a prophecy he gave *to the people of Judah* concerning Nebuchadnezzar's impending destruction of Jerusalem and the surrounding nations: "These nations will serve the king of Babylon seventy years" (v. 11). The second, Jeremiah 29:1-14, was a letter that Jeremiah had sent *to the exiles in Babylon* prior to the final fall of Jerusalem and that later was embedded in his larger manuscript. In this letter he had urged the exiles to accept their lot as captives, settle in, live life to its fullest, and "seek the peace and prosperity of" Babylon (v. 7). Moreover, he had prophesied that "when seventy years are completed for Babylon," God would bring the exiles (most likely not the original deportees, but their descendants) back to Judea and Jerusalem (v. 10).

What does Jeremiah's "seventy years" represent? Scholars who understand it to refer to an exact chronological period have suggested various
beginning and ending historical dates for this expression. Usually they are
quite convinced of their own calculations and the exclusion of other scholars'
suggestions. It seems most likely to me, however, that "seventy years," as
Jeremiah employed the expression, is not an exact chronological seventy-year
period. Rather, he intended it symbolically. Jim Edlin alerts us to the use of
seventy throughout the Old Testament "to indicate a full or perfect amount
of something."[1] He then notes these examples: the seventy nations (Gen.
10), Jacob's seventy sons (Gen. 46:27), Jerubbaal's seventy sons (Judg. 8:30),
Ahab's seventy sons (2 Kings 10:1), seventy palm trees at Elim (Exod. 15:27),
seventy elders of Israel (Exod. 24:1), and seventy years of life (Ps. 90:10).
Thus, Edlin suggests, Jeremiah's seventy years "would seem likely" to be "a
reference to a full amount of time . . . the entire time needed for God's judgment upon Jerusalem to be completed."[2]

Apparently, upon reading Jeremiah's words, Daniel was overwhelmed
with deep sorrow at the continued state of devastation of his home city of
Jerusalem. He also seemed to sense that Jeremiah's prophesied seventy-year
period was about to end. Thus Daniel "set [his] face toward *Sovereign God*
[*'ǎdōnāy hā'ĕlōhîm*]" (Dan. 9:3, AT; emphasis added). In that posture, he
prayed, fasted, and confessed on behalf of his people, Israel, to "Yahweh my
God" (*layhwh 'ĕlōhay*; v. 4*a*, AT).

Addressing God as "Sovereign" (*'ǎdōnāy*), Daniel added a double-de-
scriptive title: "the Great God [*hā'ēl haggādôl*], even the Awesome One
[*vĕhannôrā'*]" (v. 4*b*, AT). This set his God, the God of Israel, apart from any
of the gods of the Babylonian environment in which he had been living and
ministering for several decades. So, not only was God sovereign over all gods,
nations, and kings, but he was also Daniel's personal Sovereign.

---

1. Edlin, *Daniel*, 216.
2. Ibid.; see also Goldingay, *Daniel*, 460.

Daniel continued his prayer, recognizing that his Sovereign, this Great God to whom he was praying, does not stand aloof from us. Rather, he revels in a relationship of mutual "love" (v. 4*b*). My Sovereign, Daniel declared, is "one who keeps his covenant and his *steadfast love* [*haḥesed*] with *those who love him* ['*ōhăbāyw*] and who keep his commandments" (v. 4*b*, AT; emphasis added). Here, neither Hebrew word for "love" speaks of emotional love. Even though the noun "steadfast love" (*ḥesed*) on God's side and the verb "to love" ('*āhāb*) on his people's side are different Hebrew terms, in this context, both are *covenant* terms; both express *commitment* to the terms of the covenant. For example, in the context of giving Israel God's "commands, decrees and laws," Moses urged Israel to "love" ('*āhabtā*) God with their whole heart, soul, and strength (Deut. 6:1, 5). By this, Moses meant that to "love" God, a person must commit one's entire being to and submit one's entire will to the will of the sovereign God.

But, alas, lamented Daniel, we Israelites have not kept our love commitment to God our lover in this two-way covenant; our list of covenant violations is simply awful: "We have sinned . . . done wrong [NIV] . . . acted wickedly [AT] . . . rebelled . . . turned away . . . not listened [NIV]" (Dan. 9:5-6).

So, declared Daniel, "because of our unfaithfulness," in your act of scattering us (the people of Judah, Jerusalem, and Israel) hither and yon, "O Sovereign, you are in the right" (v. 7, AT; NIV: "righteous"). But "for us there is only the shame of our faces" (v. 8, AT). The Hebrew verb that Daniel uses for "rebelled" (v. 5) most frequently occurs in instances when Israel has refused to keep the requirements of the covenant to which they agreed at Sinai. Here, Daniel gave Israel's rebellion a visual quality by his use of two idiomatic expressions. In the first, he speaks of "his [i.e., Yahweh's] instructions [NIV: "laws"] that he gave *to our faces* by the power [lit. "hand"] of his servants the prophets" (v. 10, AT; emphasis added). In the second, he says that "all Israel has transgressed your instruction [NIV: "law"] and *turned away* so as *not to hear* your voice" (v. 11*a*, AT; emphasis added; see also v.

5). Here, to "turn away" or "aside" is more than simply to turn off the main path, to take a shortcut, or to stop and rest awhile. Since God had given his instruction (NIV: "law") fully to the "faces" of his people, fully visible and comprehensible, John Goldingay understands this to mean here that they have turned their backs,[3] an action expressing utter disdain for God! In other words, Daniel is saying, "We no longer wanted Yahweh's instructions before our faces!" Moreover, if a person's ears are turned away, he or she cannot or does not hear!

In Daniel's confession of his and his people's actions, we hear echoes of God's earlier scathing condemnation of the Judeans:

For they are a rebellious people,
> lying children,
children unwilling to hear
> the instruction of the LORD;
who say to the seers, "Do not see,"
> and to the prophets, "Do not prophesy to us what is right;
speak to us smooth things,
> prophesy illusions,
leave the way, turn aside from the path,
>> let us hear no more about the Holy One of Israel [lit. "cease from our
>> faces with the Holy One of Israel"]." (Isa. 30:9-11, ESV)

Yet Daniel trusts in "our Sovereign God," whose very essence is "compassion and forgiveness" (Dan. 9:9, AT), both of which are grammatically plural in the Hebrew, "suggesting deep or repeated compassion and pardon."[4] "Pardon" more accurately expresses the meaning of the Hebrew word (sĕlîḥâ) Daniel used here than does "forgiveness," since it is used in the Old Testament only of God. God is a superior, and as in our own system of law, a

---

3. Goldingay, Daniel, 474.
4. Ibid., 466.

superior, such as a governor or a president, pardons the wrongdoing of an inferior; he does not forgive.[5]

"And so," lamented Daniel, "disaster came upon us. Jerusalem, your city, was lost, utterly destroyed. We, your people, were carried off into exile. No one under heaven had ever seen such before!" (v. 12, AT). "Yet we did not seek our God's face [NIV: "favor"] nor his truth" (v. 13, AT).

For this disaster, Daniel took no issue with God. Rather, he concluded that "the LORD our God [*yhwh 'ĕlōhênû*] is righteous in everything he does" (v. 14).

"So, now, O Sovereign our God [*'ădōnāy 'ĕlōhênû*]," Daniel prayed. Then, to remind *both* God and himself of the long journey of covenant relationship Sovereign God has had with Israel, he spoke of how it all began. "The beginning," he said, "was with that mighty-hand event when you rescued your people, Israel, from Egypt. In that daring event, you made quite a reputation [lit. "a name"] for yourself, a reputation that still stands today!" (v. 15, AT).

The mention of that rescue event would recall to mind how God then had led Israel to Mount Sinai. There, in fulfillment of his earlier covenant promises to Abram-Abraham (see Gen. 17), he offered Israel an eternal covenant, which he, God, promised never to renege on his side of the bargain. Israel's leaders liked what they heard, signed up, and also promised never to renege on their side of the covenant's terms.

It seems we may, at this point in his prayer, hear a deep sigh as Daniel breathes a drawn-out, sorrowful, "O Sovereign [*'ădōnāy*]" (Dan. 9:16, AT). Then he says, "Alas, our fathers and, yes, we, too, have sinned wickedly. We have damaged your reputation! Jerusalem—*your* city, its people—*your* people, both have become an object of scorn, a byword, a laughingstock, among the surrounding nations" (v. 16, AT). Perhaps Daniel was recalling God's promise to the Israelites in the days of Moses, when predicting that someday

---

5. Ibid., 467.

their descendants, because of "their sins," would be banned to "the land of their enemies": "I will not reject them or abhor them so as to destroy them completely, breaking my covenant with them. I am the Lord their God. But for their sake I will remember the covenant with their ancestors whom I brought out of Egypt in the sight of the nations to be their God. I am the Lord" (Lev. 26:43-45).

Then, as though God might be indifferent to the plight of Jerusalem and its temple, Daniel cried out, using multiple visual terms, pleading for God to respond and act: "Hear your servant's prayers. . . . Shine your face on your desolate sanctuary. . . . Bend down [Incline] your ear and listen. . . . Open your eyes and take notice. . . . Listen! . . . Pardon! . . . Pay attention and act! . . . Do not delay! Why do I plead this? Is it for our sake? Is it because of our righteousness? Oh, No! We have none. It is because of who *you* are, my God. It is because of *your multiplied acts of compassion*! Yes, we have broken the covenant. Yet you still remember the covenant with our ancestors! Why? Because your city Jerusalem and your people Israel [*still*] bear your Name [lit. "Because your Name has been called over your city and over your people"]" (Dan. 9:17-19, AT). This implies God's ownership of Jerusalem. He cannot abandon what he owns. Daniel may well have in mind here that when Solomon had earlier built God's temple in Jerusalem, he had reminded God that he, God, even earlier had said, "My Name shall be there" (1 Kings 8:29; see Deut. 12:11). God then had assured Solomon, "I have consecrated this temple, which you have built, by putting my Name there forever. My eyes and my heart will always be there" (1 Kings 9:3).

Gabriel's Arrival (Dan. 9:20-23)

Daniel had actually finished praying, though he said, "While I was still in prayer . . ." (Dan. 9:21). Perhaps he had not yet said his amen or he had paused to take a deep breath and to think, "Do I ask more?" Just then, however, God's flying messenger showed up, arriving "in swift flight" just before the evening sacrifice (v. 21). This messenger was no stranger, for Daniel right away recognized him as "Gabriel, the man" whom he had seen in an "earlier vision" (v. 21). This earlier vision was the one that he had seen by the Ulai Canal in the Persian city of Susa, and Gabriel was the manlike one who had interpreted that vision (8:1-2, 15-16).

Daniel need not have been concerned about praying longer (if, in fact, he was), for Gabriel assured him that as soon as he had begun to pray, the heavenly response had been sent on its way, and God had commissioned him, Gabriel, to bring it to him. Of this commission, Gabriel said, "a word went out" (9:23). The Hebrew term for "word" (*dābār*) in this context, could well be translated "message" or "decree."

The expression "a word went out" occurs in two other Old Testament contexts, describing a royal "word" spoken by the Persian king Xerxes: "If it pleases the king, let him *issue a royal decree* [lit. "let a royal word go out"]" (Esther 1:19; emphasis added) and "As soon as *the word left* [lit. "went out from"] the king's mouth" (7:8; emphasis added). Thus Gabriel is signaling Daniel that he is delivering an official communication from God.[6] Gabriel is essentially saying, "Listen up, Daniel! This message is from the Supreme and Sovereign King of all!"

Then, using the same Hebrew verb twice (in this context, meaning "discern"), Gabriel urged Daniel to be aware of God illuminating his intellect and of God's voice speaking in his inner spirit: "Therefore, *discern* [NIV: "consider"] the word and *discern* [NIV: "understand"] the vision" (Dan. 9:23, AT; emphasis added). That is, "Daniel, *carefully discern* the message that is contained within the vision" (v. 23, AT; emphasis added), which Gabriel is about to uncover for him.

Gabriel's "Seventy 'Sevens'" (Dan. 9:24-27)

You will recall that earlier Daniel apparently had been reading in a scroll containing Jeremiah's prophecies "that the desolation of Jerusalem would last

---

6. Ibid., 481.

seventy years" (Dan. 9:2). This discovery had moved Daniel to fast and pray, petitioning God to end the desolation of Jerusalem and its sanctuary.

Now, however, instead of news that God is bringing the desolation of Jerusalem and the sanctuary to an end in Daniel's lifetime, Gabriel's message of "seventy 'sevens'" (v. 24) hearkens back to the severe judgment introduced in Leviticus 26.[7] There, God had warned the Israelites that in the future "if you will not listen to me . . . and so violate my covenant, . . . I will punish you for your sins *seven times* over" (vv. 14, 15, 18; emphasis added). And lest they not absorb the seriousness of this, God had repeated the "seven times" warning three more times (vv. 21, 24, 28).

Some scholars take Gabriel's "seventy 'sevens'" of Daniel 9:24 to mean seventy times seven years (though "years" is not in the text), for a total of 490 chronological calendar years. The New International Version, also taking "sevens" to mean years, translates the Hebrew passive verb of the first sentence of verse 24 as plural, "are decreed." The Hebrew form of the verb, however, is *singular*, "is decreed." Gabriel would not be one to make a grammatical mistake. In Hebrew, as in English, a singular verb form requires a singular subject. Thus "seventy-sevens," the subject of "is decreed," is a unified singular subject. Thus I understand "seventy-sevens" to symbolically refer to *the Levitical extended sevenfold judgment*, in which God is invoking his promised sevenfold-extended judgment for Israel's failure to keep the covenant.

Verse 24 is God's long-term answer to Daniel's prayer, given in condensed form. This verse does not speak to the same events that are depicted in verses 25-27. Christopher Wright sees in verse 24 God's answer to Daniel's prayer "that God would deal with Israel's sin."[8] But this answer would not be simply in the soon-to-come return from exile. "God will act so decisively that he will bring about not just a temporary restoration of a still sinful people to their land, but a complete solution to the whole problem of sin in itself."[9] The answer to

---

7. See ibid.; Edlin, *Daniel*, 228; and Lucas, *Daniel*, 241.
8. Christopher J. H. Wright, *Hearing the Message of Daniel: Sustaining Faith in Today's World* (Grand Rapids: Zondervan, 2017), 207, Kindle.
9. Ibid.

their sin would not come until some five hundred years later in "the events of the life, death, and resurrection of the Lord Jesus Christ."[10]

Gabriel says that God will bring to an end "transgression," "sin" and "wickedness" (v. 24). In their place, God will establish "everlasting righteousness" (NIV), "seal up [or, "bring to fulfillment"] prophetic vision" (AT), and "anoint a most sacred place" (AT) (v. 24). Of these actions of God, Wright says, "Certainly the New Testament writers view the cross as the ultimate 'putting an end to sin' and 'atoning for wickedness.' . . . And all these things happened (as Paul puts it), 'in accordance with the Scriptures' (1 Cor 15:1-3)."[11]

Verses 25-27 of Daniel 9, however, in my view, do not speak to the same themes as verse 24. Gabriel starts over. Admittedly, the content of these verses is ambiguous. Yet five rather specific actions can be discerned that will take place during God's extended sevenfold judgment period.[12] Gabriel sets these five actions within a framework of seven sevens, sixty-two sevens, and one seven. Scholars do not agree on the meaning of these numbers. I take these numbers as forming a symbolic framework, bracketing three periods of time: "seven 'sevens'" indicating a somewhat lengthy period, "sixty-two 'sevens'" indicating a much longer period, and "one 'seven'" indicating a very short period. None of these periods can be calculated to a definite number of years, though scholars offer differing suggestions.

The first action is the "word" for Jerusalem to be restored and rebuilt (v. 25). This does not refer to a God-given order but to the order of an earthly authority. Scholars have suggested the prophecy of Old Testament prophets or the order of Persian kings, with dates ranging from 605 to 445 BC. It seems most logical, however, that this "word" points to an order given within the lifetime of Daniel, or at least close to it. The nearest would be the decree that Persian king Cyrus issued in 539 or 538 BC, that any Jews living in exile throughout his empire could return to Jerusalem to rebuild the temple. The

---

10. Ibid., 208.
11. Ibid.
12. Edlin, *Daniel*, 230-31; Goldingay, *Daniel*, 487-91; Lucas, *Daniel*, 241-45.

Old Testament preserves an excerpt of this decree: "The LORD, the God of heaven, . . . has appointed me [Cyrus] to build a temple for him at Jerusalem in Judah" (2 Chron. 36:23; this excerpt is repeated in Ezra 1:2). While this Old Testament excerpt does not specifically mention rebuilding the *city*, V. S. Poythress points out that the restoration of temple, city, and land "were closely bound up together. The city represented the heart-beat and security of the land around; the temple represented the heart-beat and security of the city."[13] Moreover, we read God's pronouncement concerning Cyrus, given by the mouth of the prophet Isaiah (long before Daniel's lifetime): "I am the LORD, . . . who says of Cyrus, . . . he will say of Jerusalem, 'Let it be rebuilt,' and of the temple, 'Let its foundations be laid'" (Isa. 44:24*b*, 28; see also 45:13).

The second action is represented by two nouns, which I take to represent two figures, "an anointed, a leader" (Dan. 9:25, AT), even though there is no "and" between the two nouns. There is no definite article "the" in the Hebrew text, though the New International Version has "the Anointed One," referring to a single figure. The two figures appear during the process of rebuilding Jerusalem, as the reference to "streets and a trench" indicate (v. 25). Edlin suggests that streets would depict "squares and plazas where people meet and exchange goods," and this draws attention to Jeremiah 33:10-11. There, the prophet Jeremiah speaks of the deserted Jerusalem streets—no people or animals—but prophesies that the time will come when again "the sounds of joy and gladness . . . will be heard."[14] Moreover, Gabriel mentions that the rebuilding process will take place "in times of trouble" (Dan. 9:25). We have but to read Ezra 4–6 and Nehemiah 4 to experience along with the rebuilders the opposition they encountered from those who were jealous of the royal governmental support these Jewish rebuilders enjoyed.

In this second action, it may be that Gabriel was referring to Joshua and Zerubbabel.[15] In the book of Haggai, Judah's high priest Joshua and

---

13. Vern Sheridan Poythress, "Hermeneutical Factors in Determining the Beginning of the Seventy Weeks (Daniel 9:25)," *Trinity Journal* 6 (1985): 136.

14. Edlin, *Daniel*, 231.

15. Ibid., 232; Goldingay, *Daniel*, 488.

governor Zerubbabel, responding to the prophet Haggai's urging, worked together to encourage the returnees to rebuild the temple. In Zechariah 4:14, these two persons are called "sons of oil" (AT; NIV: "are anointed").

The third action is "an anointed is to be cut off" (Dan. 9:26, AT). Again, there is no definite article "the" in the Hebrew text. Who this anointed refers to is ambiguous. Some insist that it must be the same as the previous anointed (of v. 25); others, a different one. Understanding this vision as culminating in the evils of the time of Antiochus Epiphanes IV, however, I view this "anointed" figure possibly as the Judean high priest Onias III. When Antiochus Epiphanes IV became king of Seleucia in 175 BC, he replaced Onias III with his brother Jason. Jason was then replaced by one named Menelaus, who had Onias III murdered in 171 BC.[16]

The fourth action is a devastation of "the city and the sanctuary," a putting "an end to sacrifice and offering," culminating in setting "up an abomination that causes desolation" (vv. 26-27). This seems to point to the sacrilege of the little horn of Daniel 8:11-13 and 23-25 (see the discussion of these verses in section titled "The Vision," in ch. 13, "Vision Two [Dan. 8]," pp. 155-57; 161-62), which I identified with Antiochus Epiphanes IV.

The fifth action is "the end that is decreed is poured out upon the desolator" (9:27, AT). The "desolator" seems to refer to Antiochus Epiphanes IV. He ruled the Seleucid Kingdom from 175 to 164 BC, having ruled only nine years.

Customs and Practices Explained

Fasting, Sackcloth, and Ashes (Dan. 9:3)

Fasting

Fasting in the Old Testament was going without food, and sometimes without water, for a period of time for various reasons. A primary reason was to open oneself *to receive God's speaking and guidance.* Moses exemplifies this

---

16. Edlin, *Daniel*, 233; Goldingay, *Daniel*, 489.

reason with his forty-day fasting on Mount Sinai while receiving from God the law for the Israelites (Exod. 34:28; Deut. 9:9).

In ordinary daily life, however, both individually and corporately, fasting accompanied *repentance* from sin or deep grief in the face of loss. On the individual level, the prophet Elijah confronted Israel's king Ahab for his sin of murdering his neighbor Naboth and stealing his vineyard. When threatened with God's intention to wipe out all his descendants, Ahab "tore his clothes, put on sackcloth and fasted" (1 Kings 21:27; see vv. 20-27). Daniel fasted as a sign of his deep sorrow over Israel's past sin (Dan. 9:3, 5). Corporately, Israel fasted in repentance on the annual Day of Atonement (Lev. 16:29 et al.).

People fasted when in the throes of *grief.* David and his men mourned, wept, and fasted when the news came to them of the death of Saul and Jonathan and the defeat of Israel's army (2 Sam. 1:11-12). Separately, in an act of great compassion, some men of Jabesh Gilead removed Saul's and his sons' bodies from the wall of Beth Shan, where the Philistines had hung them. They took them to Jabesh, burned the bodies, and buried the bones. Then they fasted in grief for seven days (1 Sam. 31:8-13). Nehemiah, living in Susa, in Persia, received news that though it had been some years since Jews had returned to Jerusalem from their Babylonian exile, the wall and gates of the city were still in a sad state of disrepair. Upon hearing this, Nehemiah wept, mourned, fasted, and prayed for several days "before the God of heaven" (Neh. 1:4; see vv. 3-4).

Fasting could also be misused. Isaiah 58:3-5 speaks of God's people complaining to God: "Why have we fasted? . . . Why have we humbled ourselves?" (v. 3). They then accuse God: "You have not responded to our requests!" (v. 3, AT). God's reply was, "Yes, you have fasted. But while fasting, you exploit your workers, you quarrel and fight, you hit each other with wicked fists. Fasting and such behavior simply do not go together. I cannot [do not] hear your voice!" (vv. 3-4, AT).

Ashes

The expression "dust and ashes" occurs frequently in the Old Testament and in Hebrew are near soundalikes. "Dust" is *'āpār* and "ashes" is *'ēper*. The words, however, are neither synonymous nor interchangeable. An example of their use together is as follows: "They will sprinkle dust [*'āpār*] on their heads and roll in ashes [*'ēper*]" (Ezek. 27:30). What is the difference?

In the early 1970s, Professor Anson F. Rainey of Tel Aviv University demonstrated the difference with his archaeological work at Tell Beer-Sheva in southern Israel. He noted that the interior-floor material of courtyards belonging to public and private buildings was a light tan color, while the material of the streets was gray mixed with a black substance. Upon chemical and botanical analysis, the material of the streets was determined to be a mixture of dirt and an organic material (the black substance). This black organic material was identified as ash produced by the burning of tamarisk wood and broom-tree roots. "The ash left from ancient fires . . . was mixed with dirt to pave the streets." So when a mourner "sat among the ashes," that person may have been sitting in a street. In Job 2:8, when Job "sat among the ashes" scraping his skin sores, apparently in humiliation over his physical condition, he is literally sitting on ashes.[17] Daniel himself may have been sitting in a public place "in sackcloth and ashes" as he was praying (Dan. 9:3).

Ashes are mentioned in connection with grief, mourning, humiliation, and repentance. In 2 Samuel 13:19, Tamar, in deep grief and humiliation after her half-brother raped her, put ashes on her head, tore her robe, and went away weeping. In Jeremiah 6:23, 26, with the Babylonian army's invasion approaching, God advised Jerusalem ("Daughter Zion"): "Put on sackcloth, my people, and roll in ashes; mourn with bitter wailing."

---

17. Hershel Shanks, ed., "The Archaeology of Dust and Ashes," *Biblical Archaeology Review* 1, no. 2 (1975): 14, 16.

Sackcloth

This was a rough sacking material made of goat or camel hair. It was worn during times of mourning or social protest. In Genesis 37:34, when Jacob was told of his son Joseph's probable death by "some ferocious animal" (v. 33), he "tore his clothes, put on sackcloth and mourned for his son many days." In Psalm 30:11 (v. 12 HB), David speaks of God removing his sackcloth and clothing him with joy. He had apparently been sick near unto death. God, he said, had brought him "up from the realm of the dead" (lit. "from Sheol") and "healed" him (vv. 2-3). It is not clear if David's "sackcloth" was real or metaphorical. In Esther 4:1-4, Mordecai publicly wore sackcloth in Susa to protest the Persian king's order that the Jews be slaughtered throughout the empire.

God behind the Scenes

Daniel 9 gives us an insightful glimpse into the relationship that God maintains with his human servants, those who "are highly esteemed" (v. 23). We hear the angel Gabriel telling Daniel, "At the beginning of your supplication, a word went out" (v. 23, AT). "A word" (*dābār*) implies, in this context, "an answer." This was a royal answer, sent from heaven, from the King of the entire universe. Gabriel's announcement implies that the heavenly King knew the content of Daniel's prayer even before he began to utter a word. So while God allowed time, in our human concept of time, to play out for Daniel to voice the cry of his heart, God had already sent on its way his reply, his solution to Israel's sin. We should note, however, that Gabriel did not say that God had sent his answer on its way *before* Daniel began to pray. Though God had his answer ready to send, it seems that it was Daniel's *beginning* to pray that released God's answer.

Isaiah speaks of this relationship between God and his servants, but within a future time frame. In Isaiah 65:17, God announces that he will someday "create new heavens and a new earth." In this new creation, the kingdom of God will come into existence in a way that has never before been realized. In this new creation, God says of his servants, "Before they call I will answer; while they are still speaking I will hear" (v. 24). John Oswalt notes that one of the blessings God's servants will enjoy in this kingdom of God "will be perfect communication with God. In this fallen world communication with him is difficult. A hundred things arise to interrupt and confuse prayer. In his kingdom all of that [confusion] will be gone forever. When we have not yet even begun to make our request, God will have begun to answer."[18]

Faithful Living Today

In Western societies today, including the United States, where I live, there are those who call themselves evangelical Christians and yet advocate sinful practices that are contrary to the core evangelical interpretation of the teachings of God's Word. For example, some of those who are among evangelicals find no inconsistency with their faith in living together in heterosexual relationships without marriage. Other evangelicals embrace the LGBTQ lifestyle. There are evangelicals who support abortion upon demand of an unborn living baby, denying that this is murder of a person whom God has created. These sins, and others, are also advocated and practiced by many who make no claim to know God.

What, then, does it mean for God's covenant people to live faithfully in this climate of sin? We must daily "seek the face of the LORD our God" (Dan. 9:13, AT), allowing him to reveal to us any sin that we may be harboring in our own hearts. Daily we must search the Scriptures, seeking God's truth, and then act in full compliance with that truth in the communities in which we live.

---

18. Oswalt, *Book of Isaiah*, 661.

15

Vision Four (Dan. 10–12): God's Final Word to Daniel

Daniel 10:1-21

Sometime in the third year of Persian king Cyrus's reign (537-536 BC), "a word [*dābār*] was revealed to Daniel" (AT) concerning "a great war" that would occur sometime in the distant future (v. 1). This "word" was conveyed to Daniel in a "vision" (v. 1), the fourth (and final) vision the narrator includes among the details of Daniel's life. When Daniel saw this vision, he was away from Babylon, standing on the bank of the Tigris River, some forty miles east of the city (v. 4). In the vision, he encountered "a man," who, from Daniel's spectacular description of him, surely was a heavenly being, an angel, sent from God (v. 5; see v. 6).

When the angel began speaking to Daniel, "his voice [was] like the sound of a multitude" (v. 6)—a sound, as Christopher Wright suggested, akin to "the noise of a sports stadium in full throat."[1] The sound of that voice put Daniel into a deep sleep, flat-out facedown on the ground. The angel then touched Daniel, telling him to stand up, listen up, and perceive the

---

1. Wright, *Hearing the Message of Daniel*, 214.

meaning "in the words" (*baddĕbārîm*) he was about to speak (v. 11, AT). He told Daniel that he had come to help him understand "what will happen to [his] people in the future" (v. 14). Some of his message, he said, was "written in the Book of Truth" (v. 21). This book is mentioned nowhere else in the Old Testament or in any other Hebrew writing.

Daniel 11:1-45

The essence of the angel's message in this chapter is that the Persian Empire will weaken and end while Greece becomes stronger and replaces it.

Daniel 11:2-3

In these two verses, the angel covers the history of the next two centuries, during which, he says, there will be three more Persian kings and then a wealthy fourth king "arousing everyone against the kingdom of Greece" (v. 2, AT). Next will come a powerful, "mighty king . . . , who will rule with great power and do as he pleases" (v. 3). This last king is most assuredly Macedonian Alexander the Great, who finished off the Persian Empire in 330 BC. He then extended Greek rule eastward to the border of India, but died in 323 BC.

There were not four Persian kings only, however, but twelve between Persian Cyrus, of Daniel's time, and Alexander the Great. This entire group of twelve Persian kings appears to be included in the angel's use of the numerical symbolism of three and then four, "the number symbolic of wholeness," as employed by the prophet Amos in Amos 1–2 and by the wisdom poets in Proverbs 30:15-33; "its effect is to indicate complete coverage" and thus "the four kings . . . are representative of the twelve."[2] Verse 4 of Daniel 11 relates to 8:5-8, since Alexander's untimely death in 323 BC resulted in his empire being broken up "and parceled out toward the four winds of heaven" (11:4).

---

2. Edlin, *Daniel*, 259.

Daniel 11:5-20

Of the four kingdoms resulting from the breakup of Alexander's empire, two became dominant: in the south, the Ptolemaic Empire in Egypt and, in the north, the Seleucid Empire, which included Syria and Judea. War ensued between these two empires over the next century and a half, with each empire competing for control of the Middle East. Verses 5-20 detail these back-and-forth victories and defeats, identifying the ruling kings of the two empires by the generic titles "the king of the South" and "the king of the North." Each, however, can be identified from historical documents. Thirteen kings are alluded to: six Ptolemaic (South) and seven Seleucid (North).

Daniel 11:21-45

These verses give details of the rule of the Seleucid king Antiochus Epiphanes IV, who ruled from 175 to 164 BC. The events that most affected the Jews of Judea are given in verses 29-35. In 168 BC, Antiochus set out to invade Egypt (for the second time), but under Roman orders he had to withdraw (vv. 29-30). While he was away, there was a power play in Jerusalem for the high priesthood. Upon his return to the north, angered at his failure in Egypt, Antiochus turned against the Jews. He slaughtered thousands, desecrated the "temple fortress" (v. 31; see 1 Macc. 1:29-40; 2 Macc. 5:11-16). He then abolished the "daily sacrifice" and "set up the abomination that causes desolation" in the temple courts (Dan. 11:31). This was an altar to the god Zeus (see 1 Macc. 1:41-62; 2 Macc. 6:1-6).

But despots and dictators, persecutors of those who worship the God of the universe, do not last forever. God will have the last word. In 164 BC, Antiochus IV set out eastward to rob a temple in Persia, an enterprise in which he failed. Somewhere on that failed expedition he apparently contracted a disease and died (1 Macc. 6:1-17; 2 Macc. 1:13-16). This was in accordance with the angel's final words to Daniel: "Yet he will come to his end, and no one will help him" (Dan. 11:45).

Daniel 12:1-13

In a different Old Testament context, we find the patriarch Job. He has suffered great economic loss and the death of all his children (Job 1:13-19). This was followed by intense physical illness, from which he suffers unrelenting pain and community ostracism (2:7-8). Perhaps, Job thought, death would be better than the miseries of this life (6:8-9). Yet what about death? Is death really the end of existence for a human being? With no evidence to the contrary and no sure word from heaven, Job concludes that "when a strong man [geber] dies, he weakens; when a human being ['ādām] expires, he is no more. . . . When a man ['îš] lies down, indeed, he will not rise" (14:10, 12, AT). Yet still he asks, "If a strong man [geber] dies, will he live again?" (v. 14, AT).

We find an Old Testament response to Job's question rather specifically in Daniel 12:1-4 and verse 13. The message of Daniel 12 is a continuation of the message of Daniel 10 and 11. "A time of distress" and "your people" (12:1) refer to the intense persecutions of Antiochus Epiphanes IV against God's people, seen in Daniel 11, and the Maccabean revolt, detailed in 1 and 2 Maccabees. Moreover, the phrase "at that time" ('ēt hahî'), occurring three times in the Hebrew of Daniel 12:1, refers to the "time of the end" mentioned in Daniel 11:35 and 40 and again in 12:4. This "time of the end" is the period of the persecutions under Antiochus Epiphanes IV. A promise is given to Daniel's people in the midst of these persecutions that they "will be delivered" [yimmālēṭ]," or "will escape"[3] (12:1). But this escape is promised only to those "whose name is found written in the book" (v. 1). What is this "book"? It surely is metaphorical, but Daniel's vision visualizes it as containing a record of certain Jews who will die during the distant time of the evils of Antiochus IV. These will be "the people who, knowing ['am yōdĕ'ê] their God, will stand strong and will take action" (11:32, AT). Among these will be teachers known as the "wise," who will instruct others in the ways of God (v. 33). But their resistance to Antiochus's evils and their insistence on

---

3. *Dictionary of Classical Hebrew*, 5:269.

adherence to the demands of God's covenant will be costly! Because of their stand, many "will fall by the sword or be burned [to death] or captured or plundered" (v. 33).

So, how, then, was the promise of their deliverance or their escape to be fulfilled? Goldingay suggests that perhaps they are escaping by busting out of death's domain, as is explained in 12:2.[4] There, we read a clear promise of the resurrection of the dead: "Multitudes who sleep in the land of dust ['admat 'āpār] will awake: some to life everlasting and some to shame and contempt everlasting" (AT). "The land of dust" points to Sheol, the Old Testament abode of the dead in the underworld. This promise of resurrection, though undeveloped, is the highpoint of Daniel. Though God decreed physical death for humanity at the very beginning of creation, "beyond all human folly and oppression, beyond all pain, beyond all consequences for sin, beyond even death itself, God's desire for us human creatures and for all creation is life."[5]

God still has a last personal word for Daniel, as given in verse 13. By the time the visions in this book that bears his name are ended, Daniel is an elderly man. His life on this earth will soon end, and he will lie down in the grave with his ancestors. A paraphrase of God's promise might read as follows:

Daniel, though you do not know the day-to-day circumstances of the years you have remaining, as my lifelong servant, keep living faithfully "till the end." ["The end" points to the end of Daniel's life on this earth.] So, when you have finished all that I have for you to do, "you will rest." [Rest is a metaphor for death.] But death is not to be feared, Daniel, for when I decree that this world is to be no more, "at the end of the days you will rise." You will share in that resurrection with my servants who have served me faithfully. And along with them, you will "receive your allotted inheritance," which I am holding for you.

4. Goldingay, *Daniel*, 546.
5. J. Lindenberger, "Daniel 12:1–4," *Interpretation* 39 (1985): 186.

Friends, may you and I, too, continue to live as God's faithful servants until we, too, are resurrected into his everlasting kingdom.

—Barry L. Ross

Bibliography

Abegg, Martin, Jr., Peter Flint, and Eugene Ulrich. *The Dead Sea Scrolls Bible: The Oldest Known Bible Translated for the First Time into English*. New York: HarperSanFrancisco, 1999.

Alon, Azaria. *The Natural History of the Land of the Bible*. Garden City, NY: Doubleday, 1978.

Ancient Near Eastern Texts Relating to the Old Testament. Edited by James B. Pritchard. 2nd ed. Princeton, NJ: Princeton University Press, 1955.

Archer, Gleason L., Jr., trans. *Jerome's Commentary on Daniel*. Grand Rapids: Baker, 1958.

The Assyrian Dictionary of the Oriental Institute of the University of Chicago. Chicago: Oriental Institute, 1956–2011.

Barry, John D., ed. *The Lexham Bible Dictionary*. Bellingham, WA: Lexham Press, 2016. Logos Bible Software.

Briant, Pierre. *From Cyrus to Alexander: A History of the Persian Empire*. Translated by P. T. Daniels. Winona Lake, IN: Eisenbrauns, 2002.

Bright, John. *A History of Israel*. 4th ed. Louisville, KY: Westminster John Knox Press, 2000.

Brown, F., S. R. Driver, and C. A. Briggs. *A Hebrew and English Lexicon of the Old Testament*. Oxford, UK: Oxford University Press, 1907.

Bruce, Les P. "Discourse Theme and the Narratives of Daniel." *Bibliotheca Sacra* 160, no. 638 (2003): 174-86.

Collins, John J. *Daniel: A Commentary on the Book of Daniel*. Hermeneia. Minneapolis: Fortress Press, 1993. Internet Archive. https://archive.org/details/daniel commentary0000coll/page/n5/mode/2up.

Colson, Joseph. *Genesis 1–11*. New Beacon Bible Commentary. Kansas City: Beacon Hill Press of Kansas City, 2012.

Dictionary of Classical Hebrew. 8 vols. Edited by David J. A. Clines. Sheffield, UK: Sheffield Phoenix, 1993. Oaktree Software/Accordance.

Driver, S. R. *The Book of Daniel.* Cambridge, UK: Cambridge University, 1900. Internet Archive. https://archive.org/details/bookdaniel00unkngoog/page/n9/mode/2up.

Edlin, Jim. *Daniel.* New Beacon Bible Commentary. Kansas City: Beacon Hill Press of Kansas City, 2009.

Fewell, Danna Nolan. *Circle of Sovereignty: Plotting Politics in the Book of Daniel.* Rev. ed. Nashville: Abingdon Press, 1991.

Finkelstein, J. J. "Mesopotamia." *Journal of Near Eastern Studies* 21, no. 2 (1962): 73-92.

Gesenius, W., E. Kautzsch, and A. E. Cowley. *Gesenius' Hebrew Grammar.* 2nd ed. Translated by A. E. Cowley. Oxford, UK: The Clarendon Press, 1910.

Godley, A. D., trans. *Herodotus.* Vol. 2 of 4 vols. 1921. Reprint, London: Heinemann, 1928. Internet Archive. https://archive.org/details/herodotuswitheng02herouoft/page/n7/mode/2up.

Goldingay, John. *Daniel.* Word Biblical Commentary 30. Edited by Nancy L. deClaissé-Walford. Rev. ed. Grand Rapids: Zondervan, 2019.

Hartley, John E. *The Book of Job.* New International Commentary on the Old Testament. Grand Rapids: Eerdmans, 1988.

Hasel, Gerhard F. "The First and Third Years of Belshazzar (Daniel 7:1; 8:1)." *Andrews University Seminary Studies* 15, no. 2 (1977): 153-68.

Hughes, J. Donald. "Dream Interpretation in Ancient Civilizations." *Dreaming* 10, no. 1 (2000): 7-18.

The International Standard Bible Encyclopedia. 4 vols. General editor, Geoffrey W. Bromiley. Rev. ed. Grand Rapids: Eerdmans, 1979-88.

Kee, Howard Clark, ed. *Cambridge Annotated Study Apocrypha: New Revised Standard Version.* Cambridge, UK: Cambridge University, 1994.

Kerrigan, Michael. *Ancient Peoples in Their Own Words: Ancient Writing from Tomb Hieroglyphs to Roman Graffiti.* New York: Sterling, 2019.

Kirkpatrick, Shane. *Competing for Honor: A Social-Scientific Reading of Daniel 1–6.* Leiden, NL: Brill, 2005. EBSCOhost.

Kitchen, Kenneth A. "The Aramaic of Daniel." Pages 31-79 in *Notes on Some Problems in the Book of Daniel.* Edited by D. J. Wiseman. London: Tyndale Press, 1965.

Koehler, L., W. Baumgartner, and J. J. Stamm. *Hebrew and Aramaic Lexicon of the Old Testament.* Translated and edited by M. E. J. Richardson. 5 vols. Leiden, NL: Brill, 1994-99. Oaktree Software/Accordance.

Koldewey, Robert. *The Excavations at Babylon.* Translated by Agnes S. Johns. London: Macmillan, 1914. Internet Archive. https://archive.org/details/ldpd _10797913_000/page/8/mode/2up.

Langdon, Stephen. *Building Inscriptions of the Neo-Babylonian Empire: Part 1, Nabopolassar and Nebuchadnezzar.* Paris: Ernest Leroux, 1905.

Levin, Yigal. "Nimrod the Mighty, King of Kish, King of Sumer and Akkad." *Vetus Testamentum* 52, no. 3 (2002): 350-66.

Lindenberger, J. "Daniel 12:1-4." *Interpretation* 39 (1985): 182-86.

Longman, Tremper, III. *Daniel.* The NIV Application Commentary. Grand Rapids: Zondervan, 1999. Kindle.

———. *How to Read Daniel.* Downers Grove, IL: InterVarsity Press, 2020. Kindle.

Lucas, Ernest. *Daniel.* Apollos Old Testament Commentary 20. Edited by David W. Baker and Gordon J. Wenham. Downers Grove, IL: InterVarsity Press, 2002.

McComiskey, Thomas E., ed. *Zephaniah, Haggai, Zechariah, and Malachi.* Vol. 3 of *The Minor Prophets: An Exegetical and Expository Commentary.* Grand Rapids: Baker, 1998.

Miller, Stephen R. *Daniel.* The New American Commentary 18. Nashville: Broadman and Holman, 1994. Kindle.

New International Dictionary of Old Testament Theology and Exegesis. 4 vols. Edited by Willem A. VanGemeren. Grand Rapids: Zondervan, 1997. Oaktree Software/Accordance.

Noegel, Scott B. "On the Wings of the Winds: Towards an Understanding of Winged *Mischwesen* in the Ancient Near East." *Kaskal: A Journal of History, Environments, and Cultures of the Ancient Near East* 14 (2017): 15-48.

Oates, Joan. *Babylon.* London: Thames and Hudson, 1979.

Oppenheim, A. Leo. *Ancient Mesopotamia: Portrait of a Dead Civilization.* Rev. ed. Chicago: University of Chicago Press, 1977. Google Books.

Oswalt, John N. *The Book of Isaiah: Chapters 40–66.* The New International Commentary on the Old Testament. Grand Rapids: Eerdmans, 1998.

Paul, Shalom M. "The Mesopotamian Babylonian Background of Daniel 1–6." Pages 55-68 in vol. 1 of *The Book of Daniel: Composition and Reception.* Edited by John J. Collins and Peter W. Flint. 2 vols. Leiden, NL: Brill, 2001.

Poythress, Vern Sheridan. "Hermeneutical Factors in Determining the Beginning of the Seventy Weeks (Daniel 9:25)." *Trinity Journal* 6 (1985): 131-49.

Ross, Allen P. *A Commentary on the Psalms: Volume 2 (42–89)*. Grand Rapids: Kregel, 2013.

Ross, Barry. *Our Incomparable God: A Commentary on Isaiah 40–55*. Pune, IND: Fountain Press, 2003.

Shanks, Hershel, ed. "The Archaeology of Dust and Ashes." *Biblical Archaeology Review* 1, no. 2 (1975): 14, 16.

Stevens, Kathryn. "The Antiochus Cylinder, Babylonian Scholarship and Seleucid Imperial Ideology." *Journal of Hellenic Studies* 134 (2014): 66-88.

Tallqvist, Knut L. *Assyrian Personal Names*. Helsingfors, FIN: Societas Scientiarum Fennica, 1914. Google Books.

Tanner, J. Paul. *Daniel*. Evangelical Exegetical Commentary. Edited by William D. Barrick. Bellingham, WA: Lexham Press, 2020. Logos Bible Software.

Theological Dictionary of the Old Testament: Vol. 16, Aramaic Dictionary. Edited by Holger Gzella. Translated by Mark E. Biddle. Grand Rapids: Eerdmans, 2018. Oaktree Software/Accordance.

Towner, W. Sibley. *Daniel*. Interpretation: A Bible Commentary for Teaching and Preaching. Louisville, KY: Westminster John Knox, 2011.

Waltke, Bruce K., and M. O'Connor. *An Introduction to Biblical Hebrew Syntax*. Winona Lake, IN: Eisenbrauns, 1990.

Wise, Michael, Martin Abegg Jr., and Edward Cook. *The Dead Sea Scrolls: A New Translation*. San Francisco: HarperSanFrancisco, 1996.

Wood, Leon J. *A Commentary on Daniel*. Grand Rapids: Zondervan, 1973. Reprint, Eugene, OR: Wipf and Stock, 1998.

Wright, Christopher J. H. *Hearing the Message of Daniel: Sustaining Faith in Today's World*. Grand Rapids: Zondervan, 2017. Kindle.